WINES OF SOUTH AFRICA

WINES OF SOUTH AFRICA EXPLORING THE CAPE WINELANDS

PHOTOGRAPHY BY ALAIN PROUST TEXT BY GRAHAM KNOX FOREWORD BY ZELMA LONG

FERNWOOD
PRESS

FERNWOOD PRESS

P.O. BOX 15344

VLAEBERG 8018

SOUTH AFRICA

WEBSITE: WWW.FERNWOODPRESS.CO.ZA

REGISTRATION NO. 1990/004463/07

FIRST PUBLISHED 2002

THIS BOOK IS BASED ON *CAPE WINES, BODY & SOUL*, PUBLISHED BY FERNWOOD PRESS IN 1997.

EDITED BY HILDA HERMANN AND DOUGLAS VAN DER HORST

DESIGNED BY WILLEM JORDAAN

TYPESET BY GERHARDT VAN ROOYEN, CAPE TOWN

MAPS BY JOHN HALL

INDEX BY LEONIE TWENTYMAN JONES

REPRODUCTION AND IMAGING BY CAPE IMAGING BUREAU

PRINTED AND BOUND BY TIEN WAH PRESS (PTE) LTD, SINGAPORE

ISBN 1-874950-61-X

Acknowledgements

Any subject as diverse as South African wine, viewed from all directions, needs input from people within many fields of expertise. I have to thank everyone who encouraged and supported me, and who contributed or corrected the information you will find on these pages. If I try to be comprehensive, I'll probably overlook someone, but I want to draw attention to the valuable assistance provided by a few marvellously helpful people, who are listed in no particular order: Vanessa Pearce, Zelma Long, Sterik de Wet, Frans Malan, Germaine Grammar, Rob Lawrie, Di Knox, Dawie le Roux, Buks Venter, Nienke Esterhuizen, Eve Jell, Derick Henstra, Tony Gouveia and, of course, Pieter Struik, who said he wanted a book, and Alain Proust, who said he had lots of pictures. Thank you to everyone who helped, in any way.

Graham Knox

Half title page:	The main gable of L'Ormarins bears the date 1811.
Frontispiece:	The typical Cape Dutch homestead has all dwellings and outbuildings grouped in a *werf*, which is often enclosed by a low whitewashed wall.
Title page:	The vineyards and homestead at Boschendal, Groot Drakenstein.
Contents page:	The pediment of the eighteenth-century wine cellar at Groot Constantia, with its elaborate stucco relief depicting Ganymede, cup bearer to the gods, surrounded by cherubs.
Page 7:	Zandvliet Estate, Robertson.
Pages 8–9:	Vineyards near Wellington.

CONTENTS

The south-western Cape

Langeberge

Robertson

McGregor

Sonderendberge

Greyton   Riviersonderend

Caledon

manus

Walker Bay

A N

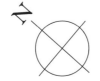

Wine in South Africa:
SOME WORLD PERSPECTIVES

South Africa is one of the largest of the world's small wine producers, making less than 3% of the world total. This figure hasn't changed very much in the last 30 years. During the same period Australia doubled its vineyard area and now exceeds the Cape's volume of wine by nearly 10%. While Australia is converting wheat and grazing pasture to vineyards, South Africa is busy removing white varieties and replacing these with the more fashionable red alternatives.

Consequently, the total area planted to wine grapes has increased by only a few thousand hectares, while the proportion of red has increased from roughly 13% in 1996 to 36% in 2001. This process is continuing, with new red vineyards comprising 80% of total plantings each year. Shortages of investment capital and good planting material are reflected in the overall slow rate of progress, as just 5% of the total vineyard area is changed each year.

Fewer than 10% of farms ferment even a small portion of their grape juice into wine, over 85% of the total crop being delivered to large wineries, co-operatively owned and run for the most part. Though the total volume of wine is barely affected by the commissioning of new small cellars, the rapid growth in the number of boutique operations is creating a larger shop window for the premium end of the market.

Steady and significant export growth continues in the traditional markets of Holland and the United Kingdom, while South Africa's own domestic consumers remain largely uninterested in wine, with just over nine litres consumed per head each year. The conversion of the middle class to wine drinking, so apparent in Australia's home market and evident also in most European countries, has not happened to the same extent in South Africa. In compensation, demand for South African wines in foreign settings continues to grow by around 10% each year. When one adds a general improvement in the quality of the better wines, which are responsible for a steady increase in the average price paid per bottle, prospects for South African winemakers appear to be on the rosy side.

FOREWORD

The South African wine industry, long a sleeping giant, is wakening. The country is one of the top ten wine producers in the world, its annual output (2.8% of world total) ranking eighth after Australia at 3.0%. However, winemaking at the Cape dates back to the seventeenth century, making South Africa the oldest of the New World wine communities.

1994, which saw the end of apartheid, energised the Cape wine industry, whose products were once more welcomed around the world. Wine regulations were modernised, allowing for the expansion of vineyards into new and exciting growing areas. Co-operatives, which in the early 1990s had accounted for 85% of the country's wine production, began to privatise, becoming more competitive in the wine market and triggering the removal of vineyards of lesser quality and with less desirable varieties. Lured by the uniquely suitable soils and extraordinary number of microclimates of the Cape, private individuals from all walks of life came into the industry to start small, exciting new wine ventures. As in Australia, California and New Zealand, the opportunities and dynamics have created a growing segment of super- and ultra-premium wines.

The presence of an enormous diversity of terroir – the vine microclimate – is intriguingly signalled by the Cape Floral Kingdom, an area that overlaps the prime wine growing regions. It has been designated by botanists as one of the earth's six plant kingdoms, hosting 5 800 endemic plant species compared, for example, to the British Isles, with fewer than 20 endemic species. This diversity of plants is due to the diversity of soils and climates that have evolved in the south-western and southern Cape over the millennia. From acid to alkaline soils; from limestone to sandstone to decomposed granite to clay; from steep mountain slopes to valleys to river beds – available soils are extremely variable and quite old.

The south-western Cape has a Mediterranean climate characterised by wet winters and dry summers. The dramatic mountains of the Cape have a significant influence on rainfall, catching differing amounts of water at different elevations; releasing it down narrow valleys; creating rain shadows and wind tunnels. Once again, a storm of variations.

Why is this diversity meaningful to Cape wines? Wine is a unique food product. While most fresh produce is short-lived, wine, through alcoholic fermentation, preserves its chemistry and character. Wine is a mirror of the soil, the climate and the human environment it encounters. With its chemistry preserved, it allows us to compare different physical environments captured by the wine, and different climates expressed by varied locations and varied weather from year to year. We can literally 'taste' its terroir.

In fact, the Cape wine industry is beginning to define its terroir in detail, in the form of Natural Terroir Units, areas that show relatively homogeneous patterns of topography, climate, geology and soil. A recent thesis by Victoria Carey of the University of Stellenbosch identifies 195 natural terroir units for the Bottelaryberg-Simonsberg-Helderberg wine producing area, which is 25 000 hectares in extent. This work, innovative in the new world of wines, is being continued by the Infruitec-Nietvoorbij Institutes, as a study that involves mapping the terroir characteristics of 27 diverse sites and making and evaluating wine from each site.

South Africa is generally regarded as a New World wine producing country, but its political, agricultural and social history place it in a class by itself. Its three centuries of wine-growing experience place it in the Old World. It has first-class technical resources – trained winemakers and viticulturists; wine educational institutes for winery and vineyard personnel and for wine consumers; research institutes for wine and grape, soil and climate; and a body of winegrowing and winemaking knowledge tied to its environment. But its technical and market participation, and thus its development, were severely handicapped by apartheid and by some of its previous internal regulatory practices.

In another sense South Africa is quite young, as its international revival only started in 1994 with the end of apartheid. Thus it joins other recently developed wine economies: California began its modern wine development in the late 1960s

and early 1970s; Chardonnay only started being widely produced in Australia in the late 1970s; Chile's premium and super-premium wines gained momentum in the 1990s; and Argentina is just being 'discovered' as an internationally distributed wine producer. South Africa is in a race with these countries – for market, recognition, and global status. But it started late and must move fast to secure an identity and position in the world's wine market. What are its resources and handicaps?

South Africa is an exciting area for the production of the best wines – whether one calls them world class or ultra-premium or just excellent. The fine, diverse agricultural environment of the Cape has enticed new winemakers, eager to 'make the best', to experiment, and to invest in the physical and human resources to do so. Since the mid 1990s a great many new wineries have emerged, most in the 'boutique' category. Such wineries bring new perspectives: they build new winemaking facilities ranging from 'state of the art' to 'old fashioned handmade'; they plant and try new grape varieties, develop styles, and revive old wine techniques. They increase competition, which in itself is good for quality.

Traditional wineries, producing well established brands in South Africa, have also been re-energised by new opportunities and new investment. Their students and young winemakers are travelling to France, California and Australia and are bringing back the latest thinking about fine winemaking. They have re-invented Pinotage, the lovely wine bred in the Cape. They are selecting and supporting the education and development of young black students, and of winery and vineyard employees, in order to bring wine, and its career opportunities, alive for these young people, and to make the human resources as diverse as the resources of the land.

The Cape wine industry is adjusting regulations on appellation and vineyard designation to be in line with those of other wine countries, so that consumers can easily understand the origin of each bottle's grapes. Regulatory change has allowed expansion into interesting new areas – Cape Agulhas, the southernmost point of Africa; the Hemel-en-Aarde valley, near Hermanus on the ocean; Elgin, a high plateau and traditional apple growing region; Darling on the West Coast, home of many old vineyards that are developing new specialities; and the Robertson area, which is moving into red wine production. Most of these initiatives have taken place since 1994.

Marketing initiatives are evolving to promote South Africa and its wines to the world. Wines of South Africa, the industry's export promoter, sponsors biannual Cape wine exhibitions, which bring in top professional wine buyers from around the world, to see and taste at first hand the Cape's diversity. It is carrying its messages directly, through winery representatives, to the UK, the USA and the countries of the EU.

Where do South African wines 'fit' with those produced elsewhere? Like its winemaking history, its wines fit between those of the Old World and those of the New World. In general the climate produces wines that are more structured and racy than the fatter, fleshier wines of Australia and California. The best have all the hallmarks of great wine: complexity, flavour concentration, balance, and length. Many are reminiscent of European wines; the Cabernets with their leather and tobacco components; the Chardonnays with tight but supple fruit; the Sauvignon Blancs with the extraordinary zip and expression of the best Loire Sauvignons. These styles – racy, complex, intense, but not excessively alcoholic or flabby – are fabulous accompaniments to a meal.

And the challenges? South Africa does not have time to waste to make its place in the world wine market. It must move quickly and with a clear focus to secure its reputation and must continue to strive for higher and higher quality. Internally, it needs to ensure the speedy integration of all its diverse peoples into all levels of what historically has been a white industry. Neither challenge is insubstantial, but this wine country is like a promising young Olympic athlete, with all the hallmarks of a gold medal winner.

Zelma Long

ZELMA LONG
ZELPHI WINES
FEBRUARY 2002

I

The Provisions of Nature

The Cape – that borderless south-western part of South Africa that was first settled by Europeans in 1652 and later became a British colony – is blessed with spectacular countryside and a 300-year history of producing wine. Its position at the tip of a continent, a mild, Mediterranean-type climate and mountainous terrain all contribute to the making of fine wines, a tradition that has seen peaks and troughs since the days of the great Constantia wine renowned throughout eighteenth-century Europe. An exploration of the region's mountains and valleys, its cellars and vineyards reveals the origins of its reputation for fine wine.

Left: The Simonsberg overlooks autumn vineyards between Klapmuts and Simondium, with the farm Babylons Toren in the centre.

Soils and climates … nature's gift

During summer the sun rises late and sets early behind the peaks in the prime wine-producing vineyards of South Africa's mountainous south-western Cape. Whether you face east or west, a range will be looming behind or in front of you, casting its shadow across its slopes. In midsummer there are some vineyards that see the sun rising above the peaked horizons only at ten in the morning. Once it has cleared the highest summits, though, the transition from shade to light is abrupt and, as if to make up for lost time, the intensity of the sunlight is overwhelmingly strong. Gabled white homesteads stand starkly outlined against the soft greens of surrounding oaks.

When one considers other areas of the world that produce fine wines, the Cape vineyards, at about 34°S, are comparatively close to the equator. On the Cape's longest day of the year, in December, they receive a maximum of 14 hours of sunlight. On the same date the sun

shines on Melbourne in Australia (latitude 38°S) for 14,5 hours, and in Bordeaux (latitude 45°N) it shines for nearly 16 hours on 22 June.

The Cape winelands, located mainly in the Western Cape province of South Africa, are centred around the towns of Stellenbosch, Paarl and Franschhoek in the 'Boland', or 'upper land', but extend westwards through Durbanville and to the Atlantic coast of the Cape Peninsula; northwards to the middle and lower reaches of the Olifants River; southwards to Walker Bay and Hermanus; and eastwards along the Breede River and beyond, penetrating deep into the Little Karoo. An off-shoot along the Orange River yields large quantities of grapes on deep, fertile and well-irrigated soils, and plays little part in fine wine production.

Positioned as they are at the south-western tip of a vast continent that spans the equator and both the tropics, the winelands occupy a Mediterranean-type climatic

3

1 The south-easterly wind, a visual indicator of summer, regularly creates a white tablecloth on the Franschhoek mountains.
2 Fog drifts into vineyards at Elsenburg.

3 The heavy shadows cast by Cape mountains in the mornings or late afternoons restrict the number of hours that sunlight falls on the vines.
4 The viticultural programme starts in earnest with the first indication of spring growth.

zone, where rain falls mostly in winter. Dry summers with a low humidity level allow grapes to ripen evenly and reliably, developing to full-flavoured succulence. About the same size as Scotland, the south-western Cape enjoys a moderate climate that is, on occasion, subjected to bouts of fury. In winter fierce north-westerly gales may bring rainstorms that lash the countryside, but in general the winter weather is not unlike that of western Europe in spring or autumn – cool and damp, interspersed with bright and sunny days that often provide a generous degree of warmth. Snow regularly dusts the highest peaks, but night-time temperatures in winter seldom fall below freezing point and frost damage is rarely one of a Cape wine-farmer's concerns.

In relation to other parts of southern Africa, the south-western Cape's rainfall is high, thanks to oceanic and topographical influences. The annual precipitation along the coastal plain, averaging 555 millimetres and

4

occurring mainly between the months of May and September, is sufficient to allow plants to grow and maintain foliage year after year. Compared with other wine-growing regions around the world, though, the average winter rainfall in the most damp of all the Cape's vineyards is low, and is less than that of any part of Burgundy, Champagne or Bordeaux. Almost all of them need at least a little supplementary water in summer to bring a healthy crop of grapes to fruition. For many vine-growers, particularly those in the semi-arid regions, a regular and permanent supply of irrigation water is an essential element of cultivation.

The intensity of the summer sunlight and the south-western Cape's relative proximity to the equator should, in theory, combine to create extreme temperatures which would be fatal to the production of good wine. Although in summer peak temperatures in the main vine-growing areas are high and grapes ripen easily, days

1

1 Most of the Cape's grapes, such as these in the Breede River valley, are grown in arid areas under irrigation.
2 Near Vredendal, lush vineyards grow in alluvial soil on the valley floor, and on the limestone hills to the left.
3 Water channelled from the Orange River is used to irrigate adjacent vineyards.

of excessive heat are rare. Two factors are responsible for tempering the heat: the proximity of most Western Cape wine-growing areas to a coast, and the 'Cape Doctor' or southeaster, the wind that blows, often with extravagant fury, across the south-western Cape throughout spring and summer.

Most of the Cape's weather, including its fabled south-easterly wind, originates from barometric pressure zones and perennial wind patterns that are continually advancing on the southern end of the continent. In summer a high-pressure zone regularly develops over the continental shelf at the southern tip of Africa, an area of warm water and unpredictable currents known as the Agulhas Bank. From this region a stream of wind, sometimes mild, occasionally tempestuous, flows in a north-westerly direction across the rows of vines with their burden of grapes towards the low-pressure zone over the Atlantic. This wind, together with a variation that blows from the south-west, dominates both the macroclimate (the weather) and the microclimate (the environment around each vine) of the whole wine-growing region during summer, its ventilating effect inhibiting the development of vineyard diseases.

The southeaster only occasionally brings rain to the coastal vineyards and even more rarely dumps moisture

3

on the vineyards beyond the first range of mountains. However, it has a moderating influence on the temperature of what, in its absence, would have been the hottest days of summer, lowering the potential maximum by several degrees. It also has an extraordinary visual perspective, being visible in the form of a seemingly tangible white cloud that crests over north-west-facing mountains. The humidity in the advancing wind, though comparatively low, condenses as it meets the thermal updraft on the mountain's face and creates a continuously flowing, luminous white cascade that falls for hours, sometimes even days, on end.

Cooling breezes are not the only benefit that proximity to the coast brings to Cape vineyards. The seas off the south-western corner of Africa are the turbulent meeting-place of two opposing ocean currents: the Indian Ocean's Agulhas current which sweeps down the south-eastern coast of southern Africa, and the Atlantic's Benguela current which dominates the climate and living conditions of the subcontinent's west coast.

The Agulhas current, flowing southwards from the tropics at the remarkable speed of five knots, or 2,6 metres per second, brings a warm-water flow into contact with the relatively dense, slow-moving, northerly drift of the icy Benguela current. Repelled by the denser,

colder Benguela water and losing its immense energy and direction, the Agulhas stream turns eastward, flowing towards Australia as a segment of a perpetual counter-clockwise cycle. As it passes Cape Agulhas its temperature is around 23 °C in midsummer. Evaporation from this warm-water mass occurs at the point where the south-easterly winds developing around the southern rim of the South Atlantic high-pressure zone pick up speed as they race towards the Western Cape's agricultural areas, carrying with them a degree of humidity to the Cape's dry summer climate.

The water off the Western Cape's west coast is as much as 10 °C colder than the Agulhas current sea temperature in midsummer, and the temperature gradient between maximum and minimum, summer or winter, remains constant at only 2 °C. In summer when the southeaster dies down, generally at night, an easterly onshore drift of air from over the Benguela current pushes onto the land a dense fog which blankets vineyards planted within a few kilometres of the chill west coast, soaking the ripening grapes as the sugar is rising in them and keeping temperatures low until nine or ten o'clock in the morning. Wine farms within reach of this ground-hugging mist have the opportunity to benefit from lower temperature and intensified grape flavour, and among the wines produced at such farms was the 'Constantia' loved by Napoleon Bonaparte and Jane Austen, and many of their contemporaries.

The Cape's mountains, apart from providing a dramatic backdrop to the landscape, play a more practical role by ensuring that the vineyards receive a good – though not always sufficient – supply of rain. Winter rain approaches the south-western Cape from the west, from over the Atlantic. The prevailing moisture-bearing wind swings in from the north-west, in the opposite direction to the major wind of summer, and collides with the ridges and ranges of the mountain chains that form barriers roughly parallel to the south-western and southern coasts. As the storm clouds are blown across the peaks they release their watery burden onto the slopes and valleys below and then roll on eastward, darkening the sky but carrying little moisture with them.

Although the valleys beyond the mountain ranges have fertile soils, the rain that falls on them is too poor and erratic to regularly sustain crops of grapes and must be supplemented. The agricultural bounty of Worcester, Robertson, Bonnievale and the Little Karoo depends on water being diverted from higher-rainfall areas and stored, to be made available on a daily basis, as the vineyards need it.

Vineyards along the Cape's west coast also need extensive irrigation. They receive little natural rainfall, as the prevailing winds all year are offshore and dry. These powerful winds move the surface coastal water northward and westward, causing an upwelling of permanently cold water from the floor of the ocean. The only westerly movement of air reaching most of the coast is the gentle onshore drift of fog that blankets the coastal lands when the dominant offshore winds die down. The thickest fogs and most intense desert conditions occur well north of Cape Town, where the offshore winds and the upwelling effect are strongest.

Sunshine, rainfall and cooling breezes all conspire to nurture the vines and their fruit, but a fourth – and perhaps most important – factor is the soil in which they grow. A healthy vine derives its nutrition from the soil and energy from sunlight, converting them into sugar and flavour components in the grape. This is a stressful task, achieved most successfully by a plant that is in peak health and rooted deep in moist, friable soil. On the question of a soil's fertility, too little is preferable to too much, for if a soil is too fertile the plant converts the nutrition derived from it into vegetative growth, enhancing its structure to the detriment of its fruit. Moderately fertile soils are best for vineyards, being rich enough to support a vine that, although retarded in its growth, has stamina to convert nature's earth-derived goodness into character and flavour in the grape.

The Cape's soils derive chiefly from the three main rock types in the region: sandstone, granite and shale. Vines grow strongly in any of them, and when the soil has a moderate proportion of water-retaining clay to provide moisture in the dry summer months, they remain healthy year round. Most of the Cape's agricultural land has a layer of topsoil containing a proportion of clay, and this in turn rests on a bed of clay. In certain areas the topsoil contains an additional proportion of limestone-derived soil that generally has better acid-alkaline balance than clay soils. This balance is carried through into the grape juice and wines. Like clay, limestone acts as a sponge, soaking up water when it rains and releasing it during the dry times.

In general, therefore, the climate, topography and soils of the south-western Cape are highly conducive to the successful cultivation of grapes for making fine wines, a potential that only began to be realised on a meaningful scale in the last few decades of the twentieth century. ✳

1 The nearby Atlantic Ocean creates cool growing conditions at Cape Point Vineyards.
2 Snow falls regularly in winter on the mountains in the Cape winelands but seldom in the vineyards.

2

Three Centuries of Cape Wines

With so many positive natural factors contributing to South Africa's success as a wine-producing country, it is difficult to establish, some three-and-a-half centuries after the event, whether the pioneers of today's wine industry recognised the land's potential from the beginning or whether they became aware of it as a matter of chance. It would certainly seem, though, that the man who first took winemaking in the Cape seriously, the commander and later governor of the Dutch colony, Simon van der Stel, knew what he was doing when he planted his vineyards at Constantia towards the end of the seventeenth century. The fact that the Cape has a winemaking tradition today can be attributed largely to him, controversial though he may have been.

Left: Lanzerac, Stellenbosch.

1

Centuries of tradition

The Constantia valley today, with its tree-shaded homes and properties, is one of the most affluent of Cape Town's suburbs with land at a premium, yet it clings still to its vinicultural past and even, in places, is rejuvenating it. The cradle of the South African wine industry, the valley was the 'grand cru' territory of the Dutch and then English colony throughout the eighteenth and nineteenth centuries, obtaining for its wines much higher prices than did the next most valuable vineyard area. It also suffered less in periods of downturn. So special were the wines it produced that its economic fortunes were independent of those of other wine-producing parts of the colony; while the Cape's economy went through periods of boom and bust, Constantia wines were always in demand.

Winemaking at the Cape began with Jan van Riebeeck, the first commander of the victualling station set up by the Dutch East India Company (Vereenigde Oost-Indische Compagnie, or VOC) on the shores of Table Bay in 1652. He planted the first vines, and in 1659 made the first wine. In 1676 the colony's first trained winemaker, Hannes Coekenberg, arrived and brought with him the first wine press.

When Simon van der Stel, the first of the young colony's administrators of note, arrived in 1679 he was critical of the farming settlers' clumsy methods of winemaking. His attitude coloured by his own interest in wine, he issued a quality-enforcing proclamation in which he assured the farmers that they would find their product '...notably improved if grapes were allowed to ripen [fully]'. Cellars would be '...visited by a committee and [sales would be permitted only if grapes were] pronounced by the committee to be of the requisite

maturity'. Farmers who ignored his proclamation had financial penalties imposed on them.

Possibly to set an example for the Cape farmers, probably with an eye for his own gain, in 1685 Van der Stel persuaded his Dutch East India Company employers to override the law forbidding Company personnel from owning property or trading for personal benefit so that he could grant himself about 900 morgen (almost 800 hectares) of forested land in the Constantia valley, beyond Wynberg. It is tempting to conclude that when he chose Constantia, he recognised the quality inherent in the deep red soils, the gentle slopes and the oceanic influence on the valley's climate. Whether fortuitous or deliberate, Van der Stel's choice could not have been better. With Company slaves at his disposal, he cleared land, planted vines and turned his property into a model vineyard. He pioneered the use of supports for his vines and the harvesting of fully ripe grapes, and employed a winemaker he had brought out from Europe. So successful was he at wine-farming that, as early as 1692, Constantia wine was referred to as 'special' and the 'best wine in the Cape'. In 1705 it sold for £20 per 160-gallon barrel, far above the price of other Cape wines. Constantia had become one of the great wine estates of the world, and the only one outside Europe.

The zenith of Constantia's fortunes was achieved under the stewardship of Hendrik Cloete, who bought the Cape Colony's most valuable farm in 1778. He established strict vineyard, harvesting and winemaking programmes that created one of the world's sweet wine classics that became known simply as 'Constantia'. Made from late-harvested, very ripe fruit fermented to around 13 per cent alcohol, this richly flavoured,

2

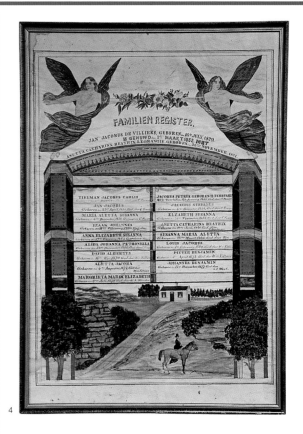

1 Buitenverwachting and the Constantiaberg.
2 A bottle of 1821 'Grand Constantia'.
3 The vineyards and homestead of Groot Constantia.
4 Family tree of a Huguenot descendant.
5 Groot Constantia's original wine cellar.

naturally fermented wine retained a high proportion of original grape sugar.

Renowned as 'Constantia' was, only one-third of it was available to the commercial trade. First the Dutch East India Company administration and then its British successors ruled that the estate had to supply one-third of each year's production for the use of the Cape government and had to ship another third to administrative headquarters, originally in Holland and Batavia and subsequently in Britain. The wines that did reach Europe via the commercial trade could be found in the courts of Russia, Sweden, Britain, France and Prussia. They even occasionally graced the tables of privileged consumers in India, Ceylon, Australia and North America. When Napoleon was exiled to St Helena in 1816 he insisted on being supplied with Constantia, and each year until his death in 1821 he and his entourage drank the major portion of both the government's allocation and Cloete's own sales.

After more than a century in Cloete hands, Groot Constantia was sold in 1885 to the Colonial government for use as an experimental wine estate under the supervision of Baron Carl von Babo, an Austrian expert on viticulture. The farm's great wine-producing days had come to an end. Its fortunes faltered along with those of South Africa's wine industry as a whole, which was almost overwhelmed first by phylloxera in 1886, and then by the effects of the Boer War. Today, winemaking at Constantia is undergoing a major renaissance, through the efforts of the current owners of parts of Van der Stel's original property.

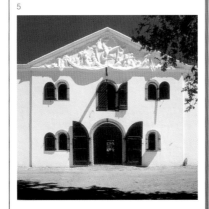

THE CAPE HUGUENOTS

In 1685, when the Dutch settlement at the Cape was just 30 years in existence, many thousands of French Protestants fled to Holland to escape religious persecution. The arrival of these refugees, known as Huguenots, prompted the government to look for alternative homes for many of them. Simon van der Stel, governor of the fledgling Cape Colony, had repeatedly requested shiploads of settlers to provide an instant farming community for his experimental venture on the other side of the world. Most Huguenots refused to consider this risky option. With the communications available at that time, people living in Holland knew virtually nothing of conditions and opportunities at the Cape. Eventually a small number of Huguenots in Holland agreed to immigrate to the Cape, on condition that their own pastor and school-teacher, Pierre Simond, accompanied them.

Although there were individual cases of Huguenots arriving at the Cape before 1688, including Jan van Riebeeck's wife Maria, Nicolas de Lanoy and Jean le Long, both of whom settled on what is today Boschendal, the first group of 21 arrived at Saldanha Bay on 21 April 1688. Between 1688 and 1700 the Dutch East India Company sent approximately 200 Huguenots to the Cape. Individual Huguenots continued to arrive at the Cape up to 1720, and the eventual total settled in their frighteningly unknown southern place was about 270 – about one per cent of the Huguenot dispersal.

Though the number of Cape Huguenots was small and their combined effect on the colony was diluted by sprinkling their settlement among Dutch and German farmers and disallowing the formal study of the French language by their children, the effect on three centuries of South African life, particularly that of the Cape farming community may be seen by the number of Huguenot surnames among South Africa's population and the prevalence of grape growing among the mixed farming practices found on all Cape farms in the seventeenth and eighteenth centuries.

Expansion into the Stellenbosch and Paarl districts

While Constantia's fortunes flourished in the seventeenth and eighteenth centuries, farmers elsewhere in the colony struggled to earn much of an income from making wine. The Cape's first European-style farms had been granted along the Liesbeek River in today's suburban Cape Town, but by the time Van der Stel arrived all these enterprises had failed. He sought an alternative location for agricultural development and found it in Stellenbosch's broad valley with its perennial water, and in the adjacent Paarl valley along the Berg River.

The first Stellenbosch farms were granted to the most diligent of the Dutch East India Company's indentured employees at the end of their contracts. Within two or three years of granting the Stellenbosch sites, all the prime land along Paarl's Berg River, in the area known today as Simondium and Groot Drakenstein, had been granted to other Dutch and German settlers. And between them, interspersed to prevent the development of an alien colony, individual farms were granted to the

few dozen Huguenot families who had arrived at the Cape in 1688 and shortly afterwards.

Many of the new farmers were inexperienced, and they began their careers with little more than an axe, a few spades and several bags of seed as start-up capital. In accordance with Company policy, they were encouraged to grow grain, trade in livestock with the indigenous people and supply food to the settlement on the shores of Table Bay. Visiting ships' crews brought a demand for alcohol that encouraged the farmers in Stellenbosch and Paarl to plant vines and make wine for sale. This market was the foundation of a major production industry that was to supply chiefly domestic needs for the next three centuries and, from time to time, fuelled the development of export markets despite the added costs and other handicaps of ocean transportation.

Although Van der Stel provided advice to these early growers, they had little capital and few skills. Moreover, a Stellenbosch or Drakenstein farmer, unlike Van der Stel

3

4

5

HOLLANDSCHE BIEFSTUK VERSUS ENGLISH WINE

The prosperity of Constantia during the period of Dutch rule should have been a model on which to pattern other Cape vineyards, but the Dutch East India Company discouraged the colony's farmers from becoming dependent on income from wine.

To the Company officials in Amsterdam the source of their profits was the East Indies, whereas the Cape, in the role of victualling station on the marathon voyage east or west, was no more than a necessary expense. Its sole purpose was to supply the Dutch trading vessels with provisions such as fresh meat and flour; fresh water, not wine, was required. Even Simon van der Stel, who eventually contributed more to the Cape wine industry than any other individual, spent his first years as commander of the colony motivating wheat production. His first proclamation was '...every person who shall plant a morgen of vines shall be bound to cultivate six morgen with other crops...'.

Prohibition on the free trade in wine was imposed as early as 1668, when no more than ten retail licences were granted. Restrictions on retailing and heavy duties remained in force until the arrival of the British, and commentators on life at the Cape often wrote about the excessive cost of wine. Levies on alcoholic beverages were one of the Dutch East India Company's chief sources of income at the Cape, yet wine production continued to be stifled.

There was a complete turnaround in attitude when the British administration took over in 1806 and was charged with promoting economic self-sufficiency for the colony. Cape wines were introduced to the British domestic market, entering it exempt from import tariffs, and by 1812 the English were drinking Cape wine for the first time. Sales, mostly of white wines, took off and within a few years represented 60 per cent of the Cape's export revenue.

3 Schreuderhuis in Stellenbosch, now a museum, dates from 1709.
4 Oriental export porcelain made for use by VOC officials.
5 A carved wine barrel at Nederburg commemorates Jan van Riebeeck and his wife.
6 *Bokaals*, or loving cups, one engraved with the VOC monogram.

who had unlimited access to the labour of Company workers, had only his own resources to rely on. And, while the Constantia farm continued to produce acclaimed wines, the administration was unhelpful to other prospective wine-farmers. Without its sustained support, any reputation for quality that they might have earned was no more than fleeting. This need not have been the case; as John Barrow, private secretary to the new British governor, commented at the end of the eighteenth century '... in Drakenstein, the wine pressed from [Muscadel] is equally good, if not superior to the Constantia, though sold at one-sixth of the price, of such importance is a name.'

The relative fame of Stellenbosch and Paarl as quality areas to be ranked with Constantia has come only in the twentieth century, following the establishment of major wine-trading companies in these two pioneering towns and, more recently, the discovery and development of valuable vineyard sites in the surrounding valleys.

6

1

Cape Dutch farm architecture

One of the world's most distinctive styles of domestic architecture developed around the desire of wealthy, slave-owning citizens of the Cape to demonstrate their social position. Thriving under a Dutch administration during the latter half of the eighteenth century, the newly prosperous elite for the most part was made up of farmers and traders. To them a grand house, like the ownership of slaves, was a badge of wealth, and the slaves themselves, skilled and unskilled, were employed to construct and decorate the edifice.

All the great farmhouses originally designed and built in the characteristic Cape style were erected between 1750 and 1840, and many of them during three distinct periods of prosperity. The first of these, from 1758 to 1763, resulted from the Dutch East India Company spending extravagantly with local businesses, prompted by fears of foreign invasion. The second, from 1780 to 1790, was stimulated by booming trade in Cape Town's port, when an unusual profusion of visiting merchant ships docked in the harbour en route between Europe and Asia, and even the new settlement of Australia.

The third and greatest period of wealth started with the first British occupation of the Cape in 1795, followed by a second, longer-lasting one in 1806. The new administration stimulated the Cape economy, wine-making and other industries prospered, wine-trading wholesalers set up businesses that flourished, and many impressive houses were built. Some of these were the first buildings on virgin sites and others were the grand development of an existing basic home.

The first houses the settlers built were naturally very rudimentary in design and constructed from tree branches and clay-based mud. As the farmers prospered they extended their homes, adding one room onto another in a row. Tree-branch walls were replaced with packed stone and mud, and as time passed extra wings were added so that the farmhouses took on the form of T-, L-, U-, H- or E-shaped structures. The walls were usually plastered and whitewashed with lime which,

3

1 The *werf* at Morgenster has many features that are typical of the period.
2 Decorative plasterwork – as here at Meerlust – often occurs on Cape Dutch buildings.
3 A mural at Uitkyk depicting summer.

frequently replenished, kept rainwater from eroding the mud between the stones. Local grasses were used to thatch the roofs and, inside, the ceilings were made of reeds with a clay overlay for protection against fire. The floors were of stone, Batavian tiles or Baltic timber, and much of the furniture was crafted from local stinkwood and yellowwood. Extra buildings for stables, cowsheds, slaves' dormitories and housing for adult children were added to form a courtyard, or 'werf', around the main house.

With prosperity came a desire to improve their homes, and when the farmers set about doing so it was natural that they should look back to Europe, and to Holland in particular, for their inspiration. Within the limitations imposed by the availability and inherent restrictions of Cape building materials and by the skills of local builders and decorators, they sought to keep up with the prevailing fashions among house designers in Europe. The shortage of architects in the colony created a demand for 'house pattern books'. The customer and prospective builder could choose a basic house shape and preferred decorative features, including gables, from a book of Dutch examples, and these standard choices were then modified according to the builder's and the decorator's capabilities. In this way, Cape Dutch archi-

tecture developed its own original look.

The gable, initially no more than the upper part of an end wall under a pitched roof, became the focal point of Cape Dutch houses. As the local artisans proved adept at plasterwork and modelling shaped edges, the concept was adapted and became a feature of the front of the house, normally moved to the centre of the original single line of rooms, above the front door. Influenced by the trends in Holland and, to a lesser extent, those in Germany and France, the designs of these gables went through stages of fashion, from simple to baroque to rococo and finally to the more severe lines of neo-classicism. The local craftsmen, too, brought design influences from their original cultures into the creative mix. Thus one finds animist and mythical figures of Asian origin among symbols of European heritage on gables and other features.

During the final years of the Dutch East India Company's rule a Parisian architectural engineer, Louis Thibault, a German sculptor, Anton Anreith, and a German mason, Herman Schutte, arrived at the Cape. Between them they provided the designs and finishes of many gracious houses and wine cellars, including Groot Constantia, which are today classical examples of Cape Dutch architecture.

1 A louvred screen separates the *voorkamer*
  from the *agterkamer* at Boschendal.
2 An outside staircase provides access to the
  loft or *brandsolder*.
3 Gables were originally simple and at the ends
  of the building.
4 The elaborate west gable of Ida's Valley.
5 A bedroom in a Cape Dutch house.

1

Boom and bust

'This colony can produce as excellent wine of various sorts as perhaps any country in the world.' These were the words of Sir John Cradock, the new governor of the Cape Colony who in 1811 issued a proclamation encouraging farmers to improve cultivation practices and produce quality wine for export, primarily to Britain. Nor was he the only one to recognise the potential of viticulture and the wine trade at the Cape. One of the world's first wine writers, the Englishman Cyrus Redding, described Groot Constantia and Klein Constantia as '... the most beautiful [vineyards] in the world' in his *History and Description of Modern Wines* (1851), and goes on to say that '... [there is] no colony where a more congenial soil exists, or where better wines might be grown'.

Governor Cradock's enthusiasm was backed by practical support when Britain, waging a smouldering war against France, allowed Cape wines to be imported at very favourable tariffs, giving the Cape farmers a fighting chance against their European competitors whose transport costs were so much lower. From 1812 until 1825 the Cape was supplying 14 per cent of the British wine market, and enjoying the peak of a boom period during which vineyard owners were able to afford the lifestyle of landed gentry. The height of their prosperity was short-lived; in the summer of 1825, just as the huge 1824 harvest began to arrive in England, weather conditions at the Cape turned sour on the farmers, resulting in a failed crop that proved to be the beginning of a slow decline which developed in intensity and gravity over the next hundred years.

At the same time the British colonial government started to withdraw the economic protection it had afforded the Cape wine industry, and by 1862 all countries importing wine into Britain were paying duties levelled at one shilling a gallon. Whereas the Cape and French farmers were paying the same duty, the latter had less to pay in transport costs, and their wines, having travelled far shorter distances, arrived in better condition.

As if this were not enough, the fungal disease powdery mildew hit Cape vineyards in 1859, reducing total wine production from a million gallons to 30 000 gallons in one year. It was soon brought under control but in 1886 another pest, the phylloxera aphid which attacks a vine's roots, caused even greater havoc, laying waste vast acreages of vineyard. Following the European example, the farmers replanted their land with vines grafted onto phylloxera-resistant American rootstock, and they gradually experienced a recovery – only to face ruin again when war broke out between Boer and Briton at the end of the century.

Virtually cut off from their export markets, the farmers had no outlet for the large amounts of wine their grafted vines were now able to produce. From the end of the Boer War in 1902 until 1918 the Cape government made various attempts to bring prosperity back to the wine trade. In 1905 and 1906 it made treasury grants to

2

groups of grape growers to maintain wine production during a critical period, an initiative that led to the formation of the co-operative wineries which still play a major role in the industry today.

There were cycles of boom and bust. In the good times the supply of grapes was comparatively small and merchants paid good prices; at other times, after concerted plantings of extra vineyards, the economics of over-production led to bankruptcy for many growers. Some diversified, supplementing their grape-derived income with revenue from fruit and other forms of agriculture.

In an attempt to regulate the wine industry, 1918 saw the founding of the Ko-operatiewe Wijnbouwers Vereniging van Zuid-Afrika Beperkt (or KWV). Its aim was to assist growers by providing advice, guaranteeing purchase for grapes or wine, establishing minimum price controls and setting up a unified negotiating system with wholesale customers. The KWV's full name, translated as 'Co-operative Winegrowers' Association of South Africa', aptly describes the body as a farmers' co-operative group, as can be found in many countries. It started out at the instigation of Charles Kohler, a wine industry leader in the early twentieth century who maintained that if the farmers grouped together to form a united front, they would be able to consolidate their bargaining powers vis-à-vis the merchants, and a realistic and stable price for their wines would result. This did not completely solve the problem of over-production – in the period 1921 to 1923 the price per leaguer fell drastically and thousands of leaguers were poured into the Eerste River – but a precedent had been set and in 1924 the KWV was legally empowered to impose a minimum price for the farmers' distilling wine. It also guaranteed to purchase grapes and wine from the farmers if required, a practice which led to the stockpiling of unsold wine and the subsequent distilling of wine spirit. Today the KWV is the country's largest distiller and the watchdog over this aspect of the wine industry, exercising control over the volume distilled and the methods used. Its own chain of brandy distilleries provides stock for much of the large domestic market.

The guarantee to buy wine from farmers and the necessity to dispose of it caused the KWV to seek out and develop export markets. Even through the years of South Africa's economic isolation, it continued to sell small volumes of branded products as well as major stocks of wine spirit in bulk.

In addition to its activities as a protector of farmers' rights, the KWV was a state-sanctioned wine industry regulator, manipulating prices and volumes, influencing wine styles, consumer education and export markets. Over the years it built up a large asset base, though nominally a non-profit organisation. The KWV owned property on many sites, primarily centred around its headquarters in Paarl where it operated a large distillery, a wine fermentation cellar and extensive maturation

halls for wine and brandy. Satellite distilleries were situated in Worcester, Robertson and other outlying areas. Dividends to farmers as a result of trading in the huge stockholdings were paid out as the directors saw fit.

Though this was the public face of the KWV, the majority of its power and influence was less easily seen. Many of the KWV directors were or had been Members of Parliament and as a group had a great concentration of potential influence on the South African government for most of the period 1948 to 1990. This affected laws and regulations and common practices that, in one way or another, influenced the standard of living and lifestyles of most people in the Western Cape during that time. The controls that had been instituted to prevent the collapse of the grape-growing industry under threat were eventually expanded into a network that threaded through every wine industry transaction and decision. It

clearly achieved its original goal and most farmers operated at a comfortable economic level, though their farm workers and dependants were not obvious beneficiaries of the system.

As the twentieth century progressed and South Africa's economic and political isolation increased, Cape grape growers found themselves supplying chiefly domestic markets with raisins, fortified wines and brandy. Although the production of fine wines began to increase in volume and importance from around 1970 – having benefited from the introduction of the cold fermentation technique in the 1950s, for example – the trade barrier of anti-apartheid sanctions ensured that South Africa's tiny domestic market remained the wine industry's only customer until 1990, when the world began to show interest in Cape wines once again.

1 La Concorde, Paarl, the head office of
  KWV International.
2 A distillery building in the Distell
  complex at Wellington.
3 Fredericksburg, near Simondium, home of the
  Rupert-Rothschild partnership in South Africa.
4 Red wine is stored in the KWV's enormous
  Cathedral Cellar.
5 The wine cellar at Distell's Plaisir de Merle.

3

4

5

1 The slopes of the Helderberg are home to more than a dozen wine cellars.
2 Carmen Stevens, the winemaker at Welmoed Winery, a subdivision of Stellenbosch Vineyards.

After 1990: a new era

The business style of the KWV was so interlinked with the practices and philosophy of the National Party that it became a clear target for change when the ANC won the 1994 elections and ushered in a new government with new objectives and policies.

From having a direct or indirect influence over everything that happened in grape-growing constituencies, the KWV was reduced to a farmer's lobby group with its retained assets. One of the biggest chunks in this portfolio was the one-third ownership of Cape Wines Ltd, owner of both Stellenbosch Farmers' Winery and Distillers Ltd (today merged as Distell) that had accrued to the KWV in 1979 as a result of its influence with the ruling party. This left the KWV as both industry regulator and one-third owner of the dominant non-beer liquor group in the country. Having some influence on regulations meant that the KWV probably played at least a small role in the absence of beer in supermarkets and what appeared to be lower taxes on wine when compared to beer.

As a result of negotiations between the new government and the KWV, the farmers' group agreed to withdraw from its role as a representative of the state. It also agreed to convert its trading activities into a commercial business, respon-sible to its shareholders, and to establish and fund the activities of a new body, the South African Wine Trust, dedicated to two objectives: the improvement of living and working conditions, and access to economic opportunities, for the disadvantaged farm worker community; and the promotion of the success of the wine industry for the benefit of all who work in it.

Within the complex of tightly or loosely linked roles and tasks the KWV once administered or performed were statistical services, now a separate, non-profit group funded by levies, called SAWIS, accessible on the Internet at www.sawis.co.za. Another KWV role was a multi-fingered grip on the supply and regulation of almost everything to do with vineyard planting. Now some of its former non-profit service centres have been converted into privately owned assets of the KWV, providing commercial services for fees and commissions.

In the past, competition was regarded as excess-ively risky for farmers and, during the KWV's 70 years of industry management, free market activity was reduced to a point where grape growers had no real access to market information or influence.

Over the years the KWV not only became an umbrella to shade the grower from misfortune but also provided a safety net in case the system failed the

3 Graham Beck Coastal near Franschhoek.
4 J. C. le Roux, another component of Distell,
  specialises in sparkling wine.
5 The tank cellar at Graham Beck Coastal.

farmer. When its statutory power was removed in the mid 1990s, the protection from risk disappeared and farming businesses had to compete in world and domestic markets of which they mostly knew very little.

During this same period, South African wine exports grew from virtually zero to become the major influence on grape growing in the Cape and therefore on vineyard composition and farming techniques. New groupings of wine producers have consequently formed and developed.

Before 1990, the SFW-Distillers-KWV financial grouping dominated the industry. Today Distell and KWV International are still two of the larger players, but many other businesses have grown out of export revenue to provide a much more competitive environment. Many of these are trading companies, or négociants, who often operate wineries but seldom own their own vineyards, preferring to invest in stock and marketing. Among these are SAVISA, Winecorp, Stellenbosch Vineyards, Vinfruco, Douglas Green-Bellingham, Graham Beck, and Natural Corporation. Two such companies, International Wine Services and Western Wines, are foreign owned and based. Kumala, a Western Wines' label, is by far South Africa's biggest brand and is among the top 10 world brands in the United Kingdom. These trading

companies are precisely the sort of non-land-owning businesses that had caused the formation of the KWV. In the absence of the old KWV safety net, however, new producer strategies have still to be developed to reduce the impact of excessive boom and collapse on grape growers.

First steps in this direction have led to new groupings among the 70 South African co-operatives, who together crush over 80 per cent of the country's grapes, and some of them have also converted to proprietary companies with grower-shareholders. However, many co-operative wineries have not reacted to the changing environment and their grape suppliers continue to provide unfashionable produce for little return.

The most obvious territory of change can be seen in the smaller site-based wineries, often called boutique cellars, which are adjacent to and in control of their own vineyards. Though expected foreign investment in small premium wineries has not really materialised, dozens of small, well equipped and well staffed wineries are opened every year and these are quite widely spread, from the previously impregnable co-operative territory of Vredendal, where until 1998 there were no private wineries at all, to Elim in the far south and even Hout Bay in suburban Cape Town, though the biggest concentration is in the traditional heartland of Stellenbosch. ✳

3

Fruits of the Earth and Sky

The essential flavour in a wine is the taste that was in the grapes at harvest. Part of the flavour derives from the variety of the grapes, for each has its own identity, but its composition, the degree of its richness and intensity, and every little nuance of its character are rooted in the energy the vine draws from the sun and the nutrients it gathers from the soil. The specific conditions that prevail at the Cape influence the flavour of its wines – as well as that wonderfully evasive measure called quality – to a noticeable, yet incalculable, degree.

Left: Graham Beck's vineyards on Bellingham farm near Franschhoek, with the silhouette of the Simonsberg in the background.

Searching for gems

Cresting hills, resting on valley floors or majestically sited below mountain peaks, Cape vineyards may be found in an array of locations within a few minutes' drive. It has not always been so; the early settlers planted their vineyards on low-lying land that could easily be cultivated. Many of the first grants of Cape land consisted of a single block containing the homestead portion on the lower, more level land where crops and vines were grown; the middle slopes where stock grazed; and an unfarmed section of the wild mountain behind.

Centuries later the valleys and lower slopes still bear large tracts of vines, but on some of the farms the indigenous vegetation has been cleared from the higher foothills and farmers, with a better understanding of the vines' requirements for good drainage and cooler temperatures, have extended their plantings upward. As an

example, at Klein Constantia there is a difference of more than 250 metres in altitude between the lowest vineyards – from which the legendary sweet wines of past centuries were made – and the highest, where Chardonnay and Sauvignon Blanc vines have more recently been planted.

The varied terrain of the Cape, particularly of its south-western corner, offers farmers a range of locations, microclimates and soils in which to grow the different varieties of grapes that produce fine wines. Vineyards may be located between 50 metres above sea level near the coast and altitudes of about 1 000 metres in the mountains, and within this range the chief factor influencing the choice of site is the availability of sufficient moisture to keep the vine healthy year round. At the same time, the drainage must be adequate, as too

1 Vineyards advance up the slopes of the Helderberg.
2 Mont du Toit, one of many boutique cellars in Wellington.
3 At Klein Constantia grapes are grown at a wide range of altitudes.
4 Glenhurst, one of the many multi-level, state-of-the-art wine cellars built on a newly planted vineyard in prime Stellenbosch country.
5 Tokara in Banhoek, which was previously a high-value fruit-growing area but is now home to several ultra-premium wine estates.

much water around the plant's roots is also detrimental.

The choice of grape variety to be grown in a certain site depends to a large extent on the composition of that site's soil and the temperatures it experiences during the growing and ripening seasons. When a new variety is incorporated into a planting programme the farmer will also consider which varieties thrive in adjacent vineyards, reaping the benefits of his own experience and that of his neighbours and predecessors. In some areas of the Cape consistently superior wines of a certain style have been produced for long enough to influence the planning of future vineyards. Moreover, extensive scientific research is being carried out to establish which varieties grow best in certain conditions and the information gleaned from such research also helps the farmer to select the variety best suited to the ground at his disposal.

Cape grape growers are fortunate in that there are no regulations restricting their choice of varieties to cultivate and, like their New World counterparts, they can plant the vines that are most likely to give them the best return. As the world markets show an increased preference for dry wines, Chardonnay, Sauvignon Blanc, Cabernet Sauvignon, Shiraz and Merlot are becoming as popular in the vineyards of the Cape as they are in other developing wine-producing countries. In addition, the Cape can boast Pinotage, a hybrid between Cinsaut and Pinot Noir, which was bred in South Africa more than 50 years ago. This unique variety brings another degree of colour and fruit flavour to the spectrum of local red wines.

The fashions of the market

The wine grape, *Vitis vinifera*, has many thousands of varieties, but only a few produce the wines that are popular among the world's consumers. In South Africa about ten of these are being regularly planted in the annual programmes in which Cape vineyards are being renewed, and they belong to the group of varieties made fashionable throughout the world by the French wine culture. Even Pinotage, the Cape's only home-grown variety, is a hybrid of two French ones, Pinot Noir and Cinsaut.

The most fashionable varieties have been popularised by the international wine trade, and growers everywhere have been encouraged to plant Chardonnay and Cabernet Sauvignon – the grapes used in France's classic wines of Burgundy and Bordeaux – in preference to varieties that are less easy to sell to the regular wine drinker. This is the pattern followed in all the New World wine-producing regions, including South Africa. Local farmer Danie de Wet, a pioneer of large-scale planting of premium white wines, has had an evangelical influence on the planting of Chardonnay vines in the lime-rich soils of the Robertson region, where every plant depends

Viognier

for survival on being regularly dripped or showered with irrigation water from the Breede River throughout the year. Today his farm, De Wetshof, and his neighbours' farms may well represent South Africa's leading Chardonnay district.

Although outwardly very similar, the grapes of different varieties have recognisably different flavours that are still identifiable in the juice after the sugar has been removed. It is these flavours that distinguish a Pinotage wine, for example, as a Pinotage wherever in the world it may be produced, although the nuances added by soil, climate and winemaking techniques determine different styles. The soils at the Cape are undoubtedly unique, but in addition to these the moderating of potentially high temperatures by the south-easterly wind, together with the remarkable degree of sunlight intensity that falls on the vineyards, contribute to the style that is distinguished as 'Cape'.

The following varieties are those most commonly planted in Cape vineyards, and they are used to make both varietal wines and blends.

Chenin Blanc, the most widely planted variety in

Above: Mulderbosch has achieved renown for its Chardonnay and Sauvignon Blanc, the latter shown here growing as bush vines.

South Africa, is used to make many different styles of wine. Traditionally the 'workhorse' in both vineyard and cellar, it makes dry whites for general quaffing as well as noble sweet wines, and it is a base for sparkling wines and raw material for brandy distillation. Its richest flavours are produced when the vine is restricted in growth and production, and it rewards cultivation as a bush vine with a noticeably fruity character. Wines made from Chenin Blanc grapes gain an extra dimension if they are fermented in barrels.

Chardonnay is undoubtedly the most versatile of all varieties, white or red. When the grapes ripen fully they have a rich flavour whether grown in warm or cool conditions, with or without irrigation, in soils that are rich in clay or in lime. They are grown successfully in every wine-producing region of the Cape, and have been made into award-winning wines in almost every one of them. Given that the grapes are grown in a healthy vineyard, the structure of the wine and the intensity of its flavour depend chiefly on the size of the crop: with fewer grapes per vine, the flavour intensifies. When fermented in a sealed tank, Chardonnay can give luscious tropical fruit

Cabernet Sauvignon

flavours, and it extracts delicious supplementary flavours from yeast and wood when fermented in oak barrels. Like any other wine, its flavour can be varied depending on whether it is fermented at a relatively high temperature or at a low one when the yeast action is slow, but in the case of Chardonnay there is a greater likelihood of success with multiple variations in the procedure. In addition to producing dry white wine, Chardonnay grapes are used in some of the base wines from which sparkling wine is made in South Africa by the cap classique method. Although they have to be picked when not fully ripe, and the flavour at first is somewhat restrained, it develops later to enrich the bottle-fermented product.

The Sauvignon Blanc variety exemplifies perfectly the maxim that wine is made in the vineyard, since the flavour in the grape on the vine carries through to the eventual wine. The best Sauvignon Blanc wines are fresh and lean, with either a grassy or a tropical fruit style, but only certain vineyards under informed care can produce these intense flavours. Some Cape producers have acquired considerable reputations for the excellence and character of their Sauvignon Blancs, but others have still

Mourvèdre

Pinotage

Malbec

Chardonnay

to find the secret of making fine wine from this variety.

Cape Riesling, correctly known as Crouchen Blanc, originated in southern France but is now seldom grown there. It is widely grown in the Cape, though, and produces a lightly flavoured, crisply structured white wine that makes a refreshing alfresco drink in South Africa's warm summer weather. Even though this variety may not be sold outside South Africa as a Riesling, its popularity in the domestic market has hampered efforts to correct the error of its name.

Riesling is the great white-wine grape from Germany, although it is currently at the bottom of a downturn in the world's popularity poll and is not grown widely in South Africa. Known here as Weisser Riesling or Rhine Riesling in an attempt to reduce the confusion with Cape Riesling, it has spicy, peppery flavours and can be made into quality dry and sweet wines that have long ageing potential.

Colombard grapes go into most of South Africa's dry white wines at the modest end of the price scale. This variety was originally planted at the Cape for brandy production, but it caused surprise when winemakers found that it produced a remarkably fragrant and agreeably fruity table wine, with more character than it has shown elsewhere, chiefly in Europe and the United States. It tends to lose this appeal with age and, as a rule, should be drunk within a year of harvest.

At the end of the nineteenth century Sémillon was

Merlot

virtually the only grape variety grown in the Cape. Today it is a minor player, its broad, rich and comparatively neutral flavours having been superseded by the more pronounced character of Chardonnay and Sauvignon Blanc. Nevertheless, the variety is due to make a challenge, as it is flexible, makes excellent wines in many areas, and responds well to being fermented in oak. Some Cape cellars are producing fine Sémillon wines.

Bukettraube is a hybrid of German origin that has comparatively high acid content at full ripeness and is suited to making semi-sweet wines. As these were traditionally the most popular wines in the domestic South African market, it was widely planted in the Cape. It is now only a minor player and its popularity is declining.

Cabernet Sauvignon is the grape that gave the red wines of Bordeaux their unmatched reputation for consistency and excellence. Although often lacking in richness, the wine has a distinct, individual flavour that allows even the novice wine drinker to recognise it. It acquires from the grape skins a firm tannin structure that softens over time, benefiting from the slow, controlled oxidation that occurs in an oak barrel. Traditionally, Cabernet Sauvignon vines have been grown in unirrigated vineyards near the coast, but more recently this variety has been spearheading the expansion of red grape varieties into inland areas dependent on irrigation.

Merlot vines were originally planted to provide a

Shiraz Pinot Noir Sauvignon Blanc Chenin Blanc

blending partner for Cabernet Sauvignon, but on their own have produced some of South Africa's best red wines. They have settled well into the Cape, and several areas that are traditionally planted with red wine varieties are showing greater affinity for Merlot than they do for its more famous partner.

Pinotage is the Cape's own variety, hybridised from Pinot Noir and Cinsaut. The grapes have thick, richly pigmented skins and produce an intensely coloured and boldly flavoured wine that benefits from oak maturation. Pinotage vines are grown most successfully as untrellised bush vines, with the best grapes coming from comparatively small plants that produce tiny crops. The vineyards are usually situated near the coast and are not irrigated.

Shiraz vines thrive in the warm growing and ripening conditions of the Cape vineyards, producing a fruity, deep red wine under almost all conditions. The wine is supple and combines well with oak flavours.

Never a glamorous variety, Cinsaut was traditionally grown in South Africa to make large volumes of inexpensive, early maturing red wine. It went through a decline in domestic popularity at the end of the 1980s and was replaced in many vineyards, but export demand for Cape red wines has given it a new lease of life. The grapes have a soft, fragile skin that contributes comparatively little flavour or tannin to the sweetish character derived from the juice.

Pinot Noir, the great red grape from Burgundy, is as

Sémillon

unsettled at the Cape as it is elsewhere in the New World, but when given special care it can produce some notable wines. Several South African winemakers are dedicating their careers to extracting fine red wines from Pinot Noir. A large proportion of the grapes also go into a richly flavoured white wine that forms the base for sparkling wine made by the cap classique method.

Fashions change fairly slowly in wine. There's normally about a decade between a show of interest in something previously unfashionable and full-blown consumer acceptance. A few years ago Viognier was unknown outside Master of Wine classes. Today, it's the new competitor to Chardonnay and Sauvignon Blanc at the top of the white wine league. Other white varieties showing glimpses of new interest are Chenin Blanc and Riesling.

On the red side of things, there are many up-and-coming candidates for future fashion leadership. The southern Rhone reds, Grenache and Mourvedre, are showing promise, when made in innovative cellars. Malbec, Petit Verdot and Tannat from south-west France, Tempranillo from Spain and Tourega Naçional from Portugal are becoming more common among new plantings and may become frequent entries on wine lists in years to come. Beyond new grape varieties, consumers are responding warmly to more and more fruit in the flavour mix in both red and white wines. Consequently, extravagant wood flavours and hard grape tannins have become less acceptable.

The mermaid in the vineyard

Vines reproduce easily from cuttings, and whatever variety a wine-farmer may choose to grow, a new vineyard is always planted from cuttings, never seed. Thus every Cabernet Sauvignon vine in any Cape vineyard is a part of one original Cabernet Sauvignon vine from Europe. Although all vines of a certain variety share the same genetic composition, being all descended from the same plant, they are not absolutely identical. Cuttings are taken only from vines that exhibit desirable features, such as small bunches or a leafy canopy.

Planting a new vineyard is not as simple a procedure as merely planting cuttings and allowing them to mature into grape-bearing vines. Since a phylloxera epidemic swept through many of the world's vineyards in the latter half of the nineteenth century, and as no effective chemical control for the aphid that attacks the vine's roots has yet been developed, almost all wine-grape vines in the world are a grafted combination of two plants.

The top half, or head, with the branches, leaves and grapes, is a *Vitis vinifera* vine of one or other variety, and the lower half, from the stem down and including the complete root section, belongs to a different species that is resistant to phylloxera and originates in North America. This latter vine type, destined to provide only the below-ground, rooted section of all vineyards, is cultivated en masse to provide a source of root material for grafting.

During the winter period of dormancy, the best scion (grape-bearing vine) cuttings are selected and pruned from living vines in, for example, an existing Chardonnay vineyard, and shoots are pruned from a rootstock plantation. The Chardonnay cane and the rootstock cuttings are grafted together, one by one, usually indoors. Once they have formed a bond, the new vines are planted in nursery soil side by side in long rows, where they remain until they form roots.

The stripling vine, with its tiny, hair-like root system, is planted out in the new Chardonnay vineyard about a metre from each neighbour in rows about 2,5 metres apart. This creates a vineyard population of approximately 3 500 vines per hectare. Some growers have experimented with high-density plantings of as many as 11 000 vines per hectare, but it is not yet clear whether significant differences are created by the lower yield expected from each vine under such conditions.

Vines may also be grafted in the field, in which case the rootstock stem is planted and the cutting of the interface is carried out on site. The stems are grafted and bound with the rootstock established in the soil.

A variation on the standard grafting technique is called aerial grafting. Thin sections of rootstock are planted and these bud normally in spring. Then the rootstock is grafted with a bud from a chosen variety.

1   Scion cuttings are trimmed to the required size
    before being grafted onto rootstock cuttings.
2   A bud has been grafted onto a growing vine.
3   The previous year's growth is pruned back to leave
    only enough for the following year's small crop.
4   In winter the extravagant summer growth of these
    untrellised vines at Bloemendal is cut back.
5   Pruning trellised vines at Meerlust.
6   The cut ends of pruned branches are sealed.
7   Grafted vines that have developed tiny buds and
    roots are sorted in the nursery.

1

The annual cycle of growth

For vines growing in the Cape the year begins in the spring month of September, when the first green buds break out of the plant's winter bark. From these fingernail-sized buds green leaves and tiny stems unfurl, pushing towards the sky. By October lush green vegetation covers the vine, and small clusters of minute flowers appear on the fruit-bearing branches. In the course of the month the flowers are fertilized and the clusters develop into the shape of grape bunches, with green fruits the size of pinheads.

Through November and December shoots continue to sprout and the plant maintains its energetic growth. If this becomes too strong and creates an imbalance between vegetation and crop, shoots are removed by topping. In a less vigorous vineyard, only the tips of the shoots are cut off. By the end of December the grapes will have grown almost to full size and the skins of some red varieties start changing colour from green to red.

By the turn of the year summer is fast approaching its full strength, and January skies are normally clear and blue. The vines receive long hours of direct exposure to the sun, and the grapes of the early-ripening varieties are nearing full maturity. As February progresses most varieties are ripening towards their peak, and the plants are trimmed to a hedge shape to allow maximum sunlight to

2

reach the bunches. This is a critical time for the winemaker, who assesses the readiness of the grapes for picking by their appearance and taste, as well as in the laboratory. As soon as the fruit is judged to be at the ultimate point of ripeness, harvesting begins. It continues through March, and as it does so the leaves of later-ripening varieties are selectively plucked so that grapes still on the vine can reap maximum benefit from the sun, increasing their sugar content and advancing towards ripeness. Those left to the very end of the harvest season, in April, are richly sweet and will be made into late harvest wines.

As autumn arrives the vine's leaves change colour, turning to yellow and orange. May sees the falling of the leaves and the first bare stems. Many of those representing the previous year's growth are clipped back in the course of pruning. By June the vines are dormant and the full pruning programme is under way. In the following weeks young vines are trained on the trellis and new ones are planted. Rain, sometimes torrential, comes to the Cape in June, July and August, soaking the vineyards and filling the dams. By the time long spells of sunshine, weak at first, return in September, the cycle of growth begins once more.

1   A sprinkling of snow on the mountains behind
    Plaisir de Merle at Simondium.
2   Sunshine lights up a young vineyard bursting
    into spring growth.
3   Pruning vines in the winter rain at Altydgedacht.
4   Autumn vines in the Franschhoek valley.

3

4

1 In midsummer, as the grape crop ripens,
   further protection against mildew diseases
   is necessary.
2 A farm worker at Asara during the harvest.
3 Grafted vine stalks are planted through holes in
   a layer of plastic that reduces evaporation
   around the young plants.
4 Traditional preparations are used by some farm
   workers to protect their faces from the sun.

Cultivating the vineyards

Two elements that are essential to the healthy growth of vines are nutritional soil space in which the wide-ranging root systems can develop, and access to moisture in the most parched of dry seasons, year after year. Where winter rainfall is both regular and sufficient, the clay within and under the nutrient soil provides a reservoir of water for summer. In the Cape's semi-arid growing areas irrigation water regularly sprayed into the vineyards fulfils the same role. In both cases, when a new vineyard is being prepared, the land is ripped and ploughed to the likely full depth of the roots, with rocks and earth being shaken loose to allow air and plant roots to penetrate the soil easily. Without this deep ripping of often heavily compacted soil, the growth and crop potential of the planted vine tend to be stunted.

Samples of the soil are analysed to determine whether the mineral and nutritional composition should be improved before planting takes place. Most Cape soils are acidic, and additional lime often has to be ploughed into the topsoil. In winter young vines are planted as grafted sections of vine stem with a small, established root structure. They bud and begin to devel-

op stem and leaf growth in spring, and by the end of summer have to be pruned, like more mature plants. In fact, vineyard management during the vines' first years is as demanding as that for mature, producing vines. The young vines are susceptible to the same pests and diseases, and need a similar spraying programme to protect them and enhance healthy growth. Weeds sprouting between the vines must be controlled, for if they are allowed to develop they utilise nutrition and moisture otherwise meant for vineyard sustenance. In winter, nitrogen-enhancing vegetation such as rye or oats is grown between the rows to improve the soil environment. These crops are cut down before the vines' spring shoots develop so that they do not compete.

Vines are naturally crawling plants and, if left to their own devices, would form low, horizontal bushes. For the grapes to develop in the shade of the leaves, and to facilitate harvesting by two-legged humans, winegrape vines are trained and tied to grow into a goblet shape, known as a bush vine. Alternatively, they may be attached to rows of wire strung between poles, a system known as trellising. Both techniques are used in the

2

3

4

Cape, and both provide support for the heavily laden vines, keeping the grapes off the ground. Trellising appears to be linked to regions rather than varieties, and is universal throughout semi-arid areas such as Vredendal and Robertson, where it allows a uniform degree of irrigation to give even growth and bunch development. Bush vines, found in many unirrigated growing areas, are also virtually standard in some drier regions such as Darling.

Given a normal size vine, and assuming that all other variables are equal, the larger the number of grapes the plant has to develop and ripen, the more diluted the flavour. There is only so much nutrition available to the plant from the soil around its roots, and this has to supply not only all the plant's cells, but also the stressful demands of the burgeoning crop of grapes. The size of the producing part of the vine, the root structure, the stem and branches, and the canopy of leaves all need to be in balance with the size of the crop of grapes that has to be ripened. To improve this balance in a vineyard where the fertility of the soil or genetic factors may cause a vine to grow excessive amounts of wood,

5

leaf or grape material, a skilful vineyard manager can trim excess plant growth or excess crop from the vine.

In addition, some grape varieties ripen more readily when they are mildly exposed to direct sunlight, and the crop from these vines benefits from a percentage of the sun-facing leaves being plucked away by hand. If excess crop is to be trimmed from the vine, the bunches should be removed long before they become ripe. If leaves are to be plucked, this should be done nearer to the harvesting date.

Only when a vine is supremely healthy and well supplied with water can it fully ripen its burden of grapes, so fading water reserves in many Cape soils during the long, dry summer were historically a handicap to the expansion of vineyards. Before excess winter rainfall was harnessed into dams, allowing regular summer irrigation in the majority of Cape vineyards, South Africa's wine-growing areas were limited to within a hundred kilometres of the coast. Now, more than 50 per cent of all South Africa's wines are made from the fruit of vines grown under permanent and regular irrigation.

1

1 The quality of workers' housing on Cape
   wine farms is improving significantly.
2 Fair Valley wine, made by the workers
   of Fairview.
3 The end of a day's harvest at Meerlust.
4 Matthewis Thabo, the winemaker at New
   Beginnings, South Africa's first black-
   owned wine farm.

Homes and castles:
some changes in land ownership

The work on a Western Cape wine farm, unlike in many other wine-producing regions of the world, is highly labour-intensive. Most Cape farms are large and the labourers' community on each is more like a village than it is elsewhere in the New World. For more than three centuries many have been the residential base for at least a dozen families, some of which have made their home on a particular farm for generations.

For most of the history of European settlement at the Cape the farm owner and his family had a paternalistic relationship with his employees and their families. He provided accommodation and the workers laboured as their part of the bargain. Only during the last quarter of the twentieth century did conditions and attitudes begin to change, both in the labourers' cottages and in the workplace.

Though the cost of vineyard land and its develop-

2

ment remains a formidable barrier to large-scale change in the empowerment of the Cape's farm worker community, there have been some rewarding initiatives to date. To illustrate the type of change in land ownership and business management we can expect in future, we look at examples of new-style, black-owned businesses and fund-raising schemes for workers and their dependants.

The forestry workers' wine brand, Thandi, is made from grapes grown in the Thandi community's own new vineyards and from grapes brought in from nearby Stellenbosch. One of South Africa's first farming and wine making projects owned and run by formerly disadvantaged labourers, Thandi is an opportunity created out of misfortune and decline.

Many of Thandi's shareholders and beneficiaries were formerly forestry workers and their families living in Elgin's Lebanon forest in a community village built by

3

4

the state-owned forestry company (SAFCOL) in more prosperous times.

In 1996, the Lebanon forestry station was closed down, jobs were lost and the evacuated community village put up for tender. As the village is on land adjoining the De Rust farm of the Cluver family, they had a special interest in finding a happy solution and initiated discussions with the community and SAFCOL on the future of the village. The result was the creation of a mutual assistance project under the name Thandi, where farm and forestry workers were assisted to establish their own vineyards and orchards on land belonging to their own Thandi Trust.

The objective is to create a profitable joint venture, making money from wine and fruit, establishing quality vineyards and a valuable brand. Though the joint venture is currently owned by a Trust belonging to De Rust,

SAFCOL, the residents of the village and the workers, it is expected that in time the farm workers and their community will fully own the business and its brand.

Thandi has already become a recognised brand in several export markets. Wine is made from grapes purchased outside the community, fermented and matured in the Cluver family cellar. The Trust-owned vineyards will in time become an important contributor to the Thandi wine brand and to the living and working standards of the Elgin area.

Further west, in the Paarl sub-region of Voor Paardeberg, SAVISA has developed a brand to generate funds from sales for social development and upliftment. Though owned by the producing company and not by the workers' community, 'Winds of Change' provides income from each case of wine sold to build community facilities. This Voor Paardeberg community own their

1 Designed by Sir Herbert Baker in 1902,
Languedoc village near Boschendal was an
early attempt to provide Cape farm labourers
with proper accommodation.
2 Workers' children dress for a concert at Meerlust.
3 Literacy and life skill classes are part of the worker
empowerment process at Siyabonga, Wellington.
The original project leader, Henry Horne, is now
principal of the Cape Vineyard Academy.
4 Life on a wine farm gives children plenty of
opportunity for outdoor play.

3

CAPE VINEYARD ACADEMY

This virtual academy has no school buildings, only one full-time member of staff, and many thousands of students spread across the entire Western Cape. Many of the students cannot read or write, yet they hold responsible positions on valuable grape-growing and wine-making farms. The Academy's courses are designed to empower these people by adding skills and knowledge to their task-oriented experience. The classes are custom-designed to align with the existing knowledge and learning capacity of the individual workers.

South Africa has nearly 500 000 full-time and casual vineyard workers, most of whom are unable to learn from the written word. And those who can read have generally had little access to self-improvement programmes. Skills development classes called SKOP (Afrikaans for Senior Cellar Training Programme) have been held in central teaching venues but are limited in scope and access. They concentrate on winery practices and most vineyard workers are unable to attend.

In recent years some consultants and service providers have offered intermittent and fragmented training for vineyard workers, but these programmes did not address the holistic needs of the workers, who are still trained to complete tasks and do not have a complete understanding of how a vine grows and reproduces.

To enable experienced adult vineyard workers to improve their knowledge, the Vineyard Academy takes expert tuition to worker communities out on the farms. These communities can apply for and receive training in technical knowledge and skills, literacy and life skills, and business practices. All courses are conducted by contracted, professional service providers, who are experienced trainers accustomed to the standards and procedures required. The courses are paid for by farm management and are available in all grape-growing regions. The sole staff member, Henry Horne, once a school principal, coordinates the learning programmes and evaluates the performance of the units.

The Vineyard Academy has an association with the CFPPA Wine School of Beaune in France, the world's leading trainer of vineyard workers. Once a year selected students from the Cape training programmes attend a two-month intensive course at the Burgundy facility to enhance their knowledge. They are placed on Burgundian vineyard properties and gain practical experience under unfamiliar conditions.

The Vineyard Academy is a bold attempt to change and improve the performance standards and personal expectations of South Africa's previously disadvantaged workers in the grape-growing Western Cape.

own small village, and vineyard development is also envisaged. 'Winds of Change' will expand by incorporating larger volumes of wines from a sister cellar in Worcester, with the worker communities in both areas benefiting from the profits on sales.

Paarl's Fairview and Backsberg as well as several other producers have land- and brand-ownership projects for farm workers. One of the earlier of these, New Beginnings, developed out of the growth pains of a fledgling wine estate in Paarl, Nelson's Creek.

'I needed my worker staff to take a more participative role than is usual in the management of the farm and the responsibilities that this brings with it,' says Alan Nelson. In 1996 this paid off with a series of medal-winning wines and Alan offered his team a choice of rewards, including share participation in the Nelson's Creek business. The farm community chose instead to

4

take land and were given 11 hectares, which they have planted with Pinotage and Cabernet Sauvignon. They have made their own wine in the Nelson's Creek cellar but plan, in time, to have their own winemaking facility. They finance their own business and have a proud record of several years of successful sales. Such new ventures invariably encounter difficulties and although the road to date has not been smooth, many more original enterprises are expected to follow and flourish.

Most of the Cape's wine workers still reside as tenants on the farms they maintain. Social conditions have changed slowly, but developing prosperity and world opinion are likely to drive increasingly rapid developments in this area.

*

4

The Cape at Harvest Time

Late summer in the wine-growing regions of the Cape is a season of intense activity, the climax of the wine-farmer's labours. In the southern hemisphere the first quarter of the calendar year is when the vineyards' harvest is gathered, when the winemakers prepare themselves and their cellars for the practising of their art. From January through to the end of March each year, rumbling convoys of trucks and trailers piled high with grapes, a powerful scent of ripeness hanging in the air, and the rich and colourful humour of thousands of vineyard workers, dominate the winelands.

Left: A fully ripened vineyard can be picked more quickly by machine than by hand.

The harvesting pattern

Ask any Cape winemaker what is the most crucial decision to be made when creating a fine wine, and most will cite judging the exact point at which the grapes are ready for picking. The juice of a fully ripe wine grape is sweeter than that of a table grape, containing almost 25 per cent sugar. At this optimum point the grape's flavours have reached the peak of their development. Full ripeness is essential for making a rich, flavourful wine, and as the summer progresses, the winemaker spends more and more time in the vineyard, tasting the grapes and measuring the sweetness of the crop of each variety before choosing the ideal time for harvesting each vineyard block. Once the decision has been made, the pickers move in, working at speed to ensure that the grapes arrive at the cellar in ultimate condition. Although mechanised vine harvesters are increasingly being seen in the Cape vineyards, they are still used less for stripping the vines of their fruit than in other wine-producing regions of the world. Here grape harvesting is still a labour-intensive operation, and in the summer months the vineyards are a colourful hive of activity, with additional labour often being called in from other areas to supplement the year-round vineyard workers. Most grape bunches are still cut from the vine by hand, placed in lug-boxes and then transferred to a large bin on a farm trailer or the back of a truck.

Grapes ripen unevenly across the expanse of a single vineyard, affected by changing soil structure or availability of moisture under the rows of vines, and even by

differences in sun and wind exposure. Harvesting teams often pick the ripe grapes of one variety in one section of a vineyard block, and then move to another vineyard, leaving the rest of the original vineyard's crop to gain sweetness. In midsummer, when several varieties reach peak ripeness at the same time, the teams spend the full day cutting and collecting bunches. This could mean spending as many as 12 hours in the field, a long stretch that is generally relieved by three meal breaks. To beat the intensity of the midday heat, the harvesters' day starts early; in the vineyards before dawn, they must be ready to begin cutting as soon as the rising sun gives them enough light.

The sun is already well in the sky by the time a bin is full, and the grapes are transported to the cellar without delay. Comparatively few farms have their own winemaking operations and most growers deliver their crops to a central fermentation cellar. Seventy co-operative cellars (or grower-owned companies) crush more than 80 per cent of the total South African harvest. Tractor-drawn trailers full of grapes are a common sight in the winelands during the hot summer months, and their snail's pace is often a test of patience for other road-users.

It is fortunate for the farmers that not all the grape varieties ripen at the same time. Chardonnay grapes, for example, have already started to gain sweetness when many Cabernet Sauvignon grapes are just turning from green to red and are still a month away from maturity.

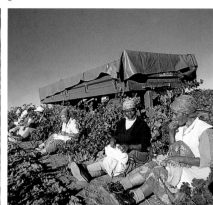

1 Restricting grape picking to the cooler part of the day requires a large team of people.
2 Harvested grapes are now transported mainly in plastic lug-boxes.
3 To enhance the quality of wine, grapes are sometimes hand-sorted before crushing.
4 Short-wave radios facilitate communication during the harvest.
5 In most vineyards, picking begins early in the day and when breakfast comes the shadows are still long.
6 Children, sometimes even toddlers, often accompany their parents at harvest time.

The different varieties ripen to a fairly predictable pattern, and this allows the winemaker to plan the cellar work so that each one may be harvested when fully ripe and then slotted into the production line. Sauvignon Blanc, Pinot Noir, Pinotage and Merlot, for example, are early-ripening varieties, whereas Cinsaut, Riesling and Cabernet Sauvignon are normally picked two or three weeks later. But there are other factors that the winemaker must also take into account when planning the schedule for the cellar. The air temperature when the grapes are ripening, the altitude of the vineyard, the size of the crop and the health of the vines all affect the speed of ripening and thus play a role in determining the calendar date of harvesting.

The first grapes to be picked for winemaking each year are generally slightly under-ripe Chardonnay and Pinot Noir which are destined to become sparkling wine by the cap classique method. These specially chosen grapes begin to arrive at the cellars in late January, and from then on there is a steady stream of arrivals until the end of March, when the last of the late varieties and small batches of extra-sweet grapes selected for dessert wines are delivered. By the end of the harvesting season autumn is just beginning in the Cape. In comparison, other wine-growing regions in the southern hemisphere are usually only midway through their season. In Chile and New Zealand for example, where vineyards are much further south, the clouds of early winter are scudding across the sky when grapes are still being picked.

6

SHAKING THE GRAPES FROM THE VINE

Mechanical harvesters remove grapes from the vine as effectively during the hours of darkness as during daylight. Although this form of harvesting is less popular in the Cape than it is in Australia, New Zealand and many of the European winemaking countries, on some farms the huge machines can be seen making their way along the rows of vines at any time of day or night.

Whereas the picking of grapes by hand is a comparatively careful operation in which whole bunches are clipped off the vine stems, harvesting mechanically is less precise. The tractor-like machine straddles a trellised row and a co-ordinated group of paddles shakes the vine on both sides, removing the grapes from their hold. A pneumatic blower blasts air through the grape skins and juice as they fall into a collecting hopper at the base of the harvester, and any leaf material is blown away before it can fall into the bottom of the bin with the liquid contents of the grape. When the hopper is full, the liquid is transferred to a bin on a tractor-drawn trailer or the back of a truck.

1 A mechanical screw pushes grape bunches into the crusher where the stems are removed.
2 At a large co-operative, truckloads of grapes are weighed before the fruit is tipped into the receiving bin.
3 Mechanical harvesters remove the grapes by shaking the vines.
4 Destalked and crushed Chardonnay grapes at Hamilton Russell Estate.
5 Bunches of red grapes being dumped, uncrushed, straight into the press.
6 Dry grape skins form a ski-slope for the farm community's children.

Squeezing grape juice

Once the grapes arrive at the cellar, they are assessed for value and then follow a selected course of treatment. In almost all the larger cellars the load is weighed before being crushed. The grower's return is normally determined by the average sugar content of the load, its weight and the desirability of the grape variety.

At some cellars sulphur is added to the grapes as a juice preservative before they are crushed, and at many the juice is chilled immediately after extraction. The larger cellars have fully mechanised handling systems at the grape arrival point, and some are geared to handle the collection and processing of over 1 000 tons of grapes in a 24-hour period. At the height of harvesting, the cellar staff work a shift system to crush, chill, cold-macerate and drain grapes and juice continuously until the pressure of grapes arriving at the cellar eases.

Truckloads of grapes seldom arrive after dark, but a dramatically busy day will see the sun set on queues of laden vehicles waiting to off-load. Every batch has to receive the standard treatment in preparation for fermentation, and the cellar will be busy late into the night.

There are certain advantages to size. In a larger cellar, wines of one variety from different vineyards can be made separately and in different styles. Moreover, the natural influences on quality that vary from season to season – like rain, wind and temperature – conspire to have a different effect on each vineyard, vintage by vintage. Thus as the quality of grapes from the same vineyard differs from one year to the next, each year a major cellar can benefit from being able to select the crops of several vineyards to obtain the best results.

On a smaller scale, most Cape estates and private wineries have several vineyards of each of the major

grape varieties, growing on different soil and under varying conditions, even though they may be relatively close to one another. Some winemakers choose to blend the grapes of contrasting vineyards, whereas others keep separate the different batches of one variety from vineyard through to bottling and provide each with unique packaging, enabling the customer to compare the different styles and establish a preference. A small operation also has the opportunity to better manage the interface between vineyard and cellar, determining optimum harvesting dates and crop sizes, and to give individual treatment to small volumes of special quality.

Selecting grapes by hand is a time-honoured first step in achieving quality. At very small cellars, such as Nitida in Durbanville and Grangehurst in Stellenbosch, comparatively few grapes arrive each harvesting day, and by painstakingly grading the grapes the winemaker can separate the marvellous from the mediocre. At larger operations careful planning in the design of the cellar affords him a similar opportunity. At Vergelegen, in Somerset West's Lourensford valley, every grape bunch is carried to the cellar in a small case load and inspected and graded on a moving belt between arrival and pressing.

Grapes for subtly flavoured wines also require special treatment, particularly those for cap classique sparkling wines that require juice without skin character. A computerised grape press can squeeze the berries so gently that when the skin breaks, the juice flows freely without taking flavour or colour from the skin. When wines are to be made using this type of juice treatment, the grape bunches are collected and brought to the cellar in small crates, then dumped straight into the press with skins unbroken. ✻

5

Making
Cape Wines

Winemaking is a creative process in which certain principles of chemistry and physics are harnessed by an ingenious hand to transform the sweet juice of grapes into an array of alcoholic beverages. Although these can all be described as wine, they vary greatly in colour, density and flavour, according to the effects of nature and the winemaker's ideals and objectives. The routes the winemakers take to achieve their objectives are as diverse as their personalities, and the results offer the consumer an endless variety of wines to enjoy. In the following pages a small selection of the Cape's most respected winemakers explain how they realise their goals.

Left: Most of Vergelegen's cellar, built on a hillside overlooking False Bay, is underground.

Glimpses into some Cape cellars

Wine cellars are like signatures; no two are alike. The cellarmaster's requirements are so individual that the size and composition of each one's domain are unique. The only factor common to all cellars is the need to protect the flavour that the soil and the environment have given to the grape, and to reproduce it in the wine. This need drives all choices related to the location of the cellar, its size and its accessibility. In the vineyard, retaining all the desired qualities of the grape in the eventual wine is the factor determining the number of grapes that are allowed to ripen on each vine and the date or hour of harvesting each block. The same factor plays a vital role in the design and construction of a cellar, determining its scale and format.

Many cellars can handle the complete winemaking process, from pressing the grapes when they arrive to labelling the bottles of wine. Others are equipped only

for pressing the grapes and fermenting the juice, as it was a common practice in the past for farmers merely to proceed so far and then send the resulting wine to a wholesaler to be blended and matured.

Among those cellars that do make their own wine, some are tiny, barely larger than a double garage, whereas others may cover a hectare. Whatever its extent, when a cellar is being planned there are two basic rules to be borne in mind. The first is that there should be a natural progression from the arrival of the grapes through the stages of juice processing, fermentation and maturation to the bottling and then shipment of the wine. A steady, even flow – from the grapes arriving intact at one side of the cellar to the final product leaving from the other – helps to ensure that the goodness extracted from the vineyard is carried through into the bottle.

The second rule involves making maximum use of

1 & 3 Two contrasting views of the Spice Route
cellar: in the second picture the grape skins are
being punched down through the cap.
2 Mainly French and American oak are used for
maturation barrels.

gravity when liquid is being transferred from stage to stage. It is believed that wine loses flavour when it is pumped, and although virtually all wine is moved by mechanical means at some time or another in the course of its making, cellarmasters prefer to keep such treatment to a minimum and rather allow the wine to move by means of gravitational flow. The Cape's geography, which allows cellars to be built on and into sloping ground, provides the ideal platform for this principle. Examples of its use can be clearly seen in cellars such as Morgenhof and Vergelegen, where the barrel storage cellar is below the fermentation tank level.

The actual process of making wine can be said to begin with the crushing of the grapes. This can be done to varying degrees: at one extreme the grapes are tumbled helter-skelter into the crusher and macerated, then compressed to extract the maximum amount of juice.

3

Sometimes whole bunches of unbroken grapes are squeezed more gently and the most delicately flavoured juice is kept separate from liquid with a more robust character that is derived from near the skin tissue of the berry. At other times again, the juice of uncrushed and unpressed grapes is fermented by yeast cells that penetrate the skin. This procedure, which takes place in an enclosed tank and is known as anaerobic fermentation, is commonly used to make Beaujolais wines in France and also occasionally in the Cape.

The rich, succulent flavours of premium wines are fragile, requiring protection from summer heat and the potential ravages of oxygen. All South African cellars contain cooling equipment and closed tanks that allow wines to be fermented at a desired speed and at any temperature. The lower the temperature, the slower the rate of fermentation.

1 Cordoba is an example of a small modern
   winery at the Cape.
2 Wine maturing in barrels and bottles in a
   temperature-controlled cellar.
3 Immediately after bottling, there is little spare
   floor space in a modern winery.
4 Etienne le Riche, the owner and cellarmaster
   of Le Riche winery.

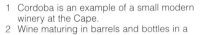

White wines are produced from only the juice of the grape, although the skins of white grapes, lacking any obvious colour, are sometimes steeped in the juice to add flavour. Generally, though, grape husks play little or no role in making white wines. Yeast added to the juice converts the grape's natural sugar into alcohol and carbon dioxide during the fermentation process. White wine may be bottled soon after it emerges from the fermentation vessel (tank or barrel), or it may be allowed to mature further in wood. As the accounts in the following pages will show, each winemaker uses his or her experience and imagination to make the most of the resources available and produce an original series of masterpieces.

Rosé wines are made in the same way as white wines. The classic rosé type, blanc de noir, is made from the clear juice of red grapes that is lightly stained by the colour in the broken skins before the juice is drained off.

Alternatively, rosé wines may be made simply by blending white and red wines.

Sparkling wines are created by incorporating carbon dioxide into a still wine, and this may be achieved through a number of different techniques. In the Cape one of the more popular means used is the making of bottle-fermented cap classique, following the méthode champenoise, which derives from the Champagne region of France. In this method, a mixture of fermented wine, sugar and yeast is bottled and sealed. The yeast ferments the sugar in the blend, creating carbon dioxide, which dissolves in the wine and adds a little more alcohol at the same time. At this stage the bottle contains a full-bodied wine, carbon dioxide at about six atmospheres of pressure, and a layer of dormant yeast deposited on the lower surface of the bottle.

A vital task for cap classique producers is to remove

1 In the cellar at Twee Jonge Gezellen, cap classique sparkling wine ferments steadily.
2 Concrete fermentation tanks and maturation barrels at Linton Park.
3 A proportion of South Africa's wine barrels are made locally from imported wood.

the yeast without losing anything of value from the wine. This is achieved by using gravity to shake the yeast down the side of the bottle into the neck of the inverted bottle, where it forms a small, flat cake on the cap. When the bottle is reversed and opened, the gas pressure blows the cake out, leaving the dissolved contents intact, and with a retained pressure of about four atmospheres. A small volume of wine with sugar dissolved in it is normally added to replace the liquid lost when the yeast was removed, and to balance the flavour with its comparatively high acid content.

Colour and an additional dimension of flavour are given to red wines by the inclusion of red grape skins when the juice is fermenting. To extract the maximum desired colour and flavour components from the skins, red winemaking involves special equipment and treatment during and after fermentation. Whereas fermenting white wine is a virtually pure liquid, red wine in its

2

formative stage contains a bulky mass of red grape skins. It has to be fermented in a wide-mouthed container that will allow the mountain of skins to be removed after the liquid wine has been drained off.

Fine red wines are normally matured in oak barrels. Between the alcohol-producing stage of fermentation and the long resting period known as maturation, most red wines go through a second fermentation, during which some of the minute volume of malic acid they contain is converted into lactic acid. This malolactic fermentation modifies the wine's flavour, adding softness and roundness, and normally occurs in tanks before the wine is transferred into barrels. Some winemakers, however, prefer to move the wine into barrels directly after first-stage fermentation, and the malolactic fermentation takes place in the barrels. It is normal practice for a red wine to remain in oak for between six months and two years before it is bottled.

3

BARRELS AND COOPERING

Long before glass bottles were invented, wine was stored and transported in wooden barrels, and coopering was an important industry throughout Europe. Even in those times there was a major commercial market in wines, and the grape growers of Spain, Italy, Portugal, Germany and France supplied wine to their domestic and export markets – the latter chiefly in western Europe – in small, manageable barrels. This was the practice from the fifteenth century until the twentieth, and even as recently as 60 years ago, more wine was shipped for export in barrels than in bottles.

Historically, many different woods were used to make wine barrels, but oak was reliable in many ways and became the preferred material, particularly in France. In time, after glass and ceramic bottles and then steel tanks were invented, the use of oak barrels for storage and for maturation declined, and by the second half of the twentieth century was comparatively limited. Wine lovers then discovered that in many cases they preferred the taste of wine that had spent a formative time in casks made from the oak tree and the use of oak barrels for wine production increased again.

There are many theories about what happens to wine in an oak barrel. All that is known for certain is that many youthful wines gain not only a more lively flavour and richer colour, but also the ability to retain these qualities for a longer period than an equivalent wine that has not been in wood.

Oak barrels for winemaking are manufactured in Europe and in the United States of America, areas home to different species of oak tree. The European oak has porous wood that must be split into wooden staves along the grain for a water- or wine-tight barrel to be made. The tubular effect of the wood's molecular structure must not allow wine to pass sideways through the stave. This restriction means that only 20 per cent of a perfect tree can be used for coopering, and naturally this influences the cost of the barrels.

The wood of American oak trees is less porous, and can be sawn into planks, even across the grain, and then cut into staves that are used for barrel-making. It imparts a more pronounced flavour to the wine than does the European oak, giving winemakers an additional element to consider when deciding on their preferred wine style.

Oak trees also grow in South Africa, having been brought into the country at the time of the early European settlement. They add decorative effect to the countryside, but their fast-growing timber is too porous for use in barrel-making. Consequently all timber for cask construction in South Africa is imported, either in the form of staves ready for assembly, or as completed barrels.

After felling, the giant oak tree chosen for barrel-making lies on the ground it has overshadowed for more than two centuries. The massive trunk is sawn into barrel-length cylinders and these are split lengthwise into rough planks about a hand-span wide. Each will be trimmed to make a barrel stave. These planks are stacked high on pallets in the open air and left for several years to season in the sun and rain. The sap leaches out of the timber and the moisture content of the wood drops to that of the surrounding air.

To make a barrel, these rectangular staves are tapered at each end. About 30 of them are stood on one end and grouped in the form of a barrel, then held in place by iron hoops. To bend the oak into a curve, one side of the staves is exposed to a small wood fire. When hot, the lower ends of the grouped staves are winched or jacked together to create the barrel unit and other iron hoops are hammered into place to hold the staves in this new shape.

The initial heating of the stave creates a lightly singed appearance and gives a mildly toasted flavour to wine stored later in the barrel. Most coopers give the tubular shape a further degree of toasting over a fire at this stage of assembly. Then the circular ends of the barrel are inserted, the working iron hoops are replaced with new galvanised hoops to hold the staves tightly in place, and the barrel's exterior is sanded clean. Finally, water is pumped into the new barrel and the pressure inside is raised to several times that of the atmosphere. When the barrel shows no sign of leaking, it is packed for shipment to a winery.

1

Vine by vine

La Motte

'Making wine is a team thing,' says Jacques Borman of La Motte, in the Franschhoek valley. 'It's fantastic when you have responsible people to work with, like we have here. I can ask my team to come in on Easter Sunday night at 11 p.m. to help me, and then choose two from the group who offer. And that's on a farm where Easter is an important event. If you have that kind of work relationship, everything's a pleasure.'

There are more than 100 hectares of vineyard at La Motte, and the farm incorporates a small village of about 50 families. The men and women of the community are mostly employed in the estate's vineyards and cellar, and many have lived and worked in the same place for more than 15 years. The next stage in the plans for the community is the establishment of a retirement home on the farm.

'The most important asset we have is the right workforce,' says Jacques. 'And this comes from a long-term plan. You can't train a person to trellis vines in a year. Or how to work with canopy management. For this we need an ongoing programme. We send our staff on a lot of training courses where they learn things like how to do a better job when spraying, or trellising techniques for different varieties. They bring back many new ideas which benefit everybody here.'

Pietie le Roux is the vineyard manager at La Motte and directs the viticultural programme.

'What we're aiming at is that the place can run itself,' explains Pietie. 'When both Jacques and I had to be away from the estate for a couple of weeks, the team here ran the whole farm on their own. When you can do that, when they run the farm better than you could have done, that's great.'

La Motte is an example of people harnessing nature and directing it towards an objective. With three widely varying soil types within its boundaries, this farm is

2

1 At La Motte, every row of vines is individually
  monitored, all year long.
2 Winemaker Jacques Borman encourages all farm
  workers to evaluate the cellar's young wines.
3 La Motte's homestead is perfectly proportioned
  and immaculately kept.
4 The tasting room adjoins the humidity-controlled
  barrel cellar.
5 Pietie le Roux, La Motte's viticulturist, has a highly
  trained team of vineyard workers.

comparatively difficult to cultivate and requires understanding, planning and careful treatment by informed
people, in this case, the entire workforce. It encompasses
roughly equal areas of granitic, loamy soil with a high
clay content, low-fertility sandy soil with a clay underlay-
er, and fertile riverbank alluvials. To provide the estate
cellar with a consistent supply of premium quality
grapes from all parts of the farm, Pietie's staff implement
a comprehensive, differentiated programme for each
block, and in many cases the treatment varies from one
row of vines to the next.

The objective of this painstaking programme is to
produce balanced, richly flavoured wines. Without
speedy harvesting at the ideal point of ripeness, block by
block, much of the value of the year's work would be
lost.

Even after the grapes have been picked and the wine
is being made, Jacques involves his team in evaluating

the product during maturation to help co-ordinate their
understanding and effort.

'We bring everyone working on the farm into the
winery about two weeks after the last load of grapes has
been offloaded and we start the tasting with the
Sauvignon Blancs. Each tank of this sensitive variety is
identified as to the block of vines it came from. Our
workers can then taste the differences between blocks
treated in different ways. And we repeat this process with
every variety. Later in the year, we go through the whole
thing again to see how each wine has developed.'

Each year the La Motte team experiments with yeast
strains and fermentation techniques to vary flavours
according to an individual vineyard's special characteristics. Thus vineyard and cellar workers are united in their
efforts to constantly improve their product.

Different personalities

Klein Constantia

'We have to treat all our white grape varieties very differently to end up with the flavours we want in the bottle,' says Ross Gower of Klein Constantia Estate. 'In the winemaking process, Sauvignon Blanc doesn't really add to the flavours you find in the vineyard at picking time. On the other hand, all the richness and fruit flavours of Chardonnay tend to develop with stimulation and time in the treatment you give it in the cellar.

'While you have to be ultra careful with Sauvignon Blanc and keep it away from air and oxygen, Chardonnay thrives on open-handed treatment. We give our Sauvignon Blanc grapes a dose of sulphur at the crusher as the first stage of protection against the potentially harmful effects of oxygen. Chardonnay first meets up with sulphur only when it comes out of the barrels, after it's been in the cellar for about eight months and has benefited a lot from controlled contact with oxygen.'

A third white variety made at Klein Constantia needs different treatment again.

'By contrast, Riesling has its own original programme.' Ross explains: 'All of our white grapes develop high acidity in the vineyard. While we lose some of the natural acidity in Sauvignon Blanc and Chardonnay in a deliberate programme of skin contact after crushing, we can't do that with Riesling. Our Riesling comes into the cellar with high acidity and a percentage of noble rot. We crush the grapes and separate the juice from the skins as fast as possible so that we don't pick up any unwanted flavours. And I have to have a short fermentation, removing the yeast while there's still some sugar present, to make sure we have a balanced wine.'

Ross ferments the Sauvignon Blanc carefully at a slow, controlled rate and at a low temperature in stainless steel tanks. Meanwhile, in another part of the cellar, the fermentation of Chardonnay is started in a tank at a warm temperature and the liquid is then chilled to make the yeast inactive. The new must is pumped into 500-litre barrels where it warms up rapidly and the fermentation process continues at a temperature of about 20 °C until there is no sugar left.

'We then top up the barrels and wait for malolactic fermentation to begin of its own accord,' continues Ross. 'When that is finished we gently stir the wine to remove carbon dioxide, and make sure that all the barrels are full

3

1 False Bay has a moderating influence on vineyard
  temperature at Klein Constantia.
2 Ross Gower, the estate's cellarmaster since 1984.
3 Although only minutes from suburban Cape Town,
  Klein Constantia has a distinctly rural atmosphere.
4 Leaf cover around bunches is reduced before harvest.
5 The neo-classical homestead dates from the 1790s.
6 Visitors sample the estate's wine in the modern tasting
  and sales room.

4

before sealing them for a couple of months of maturation. During this period we stir up the lees that is at the
bottom of each barrel every two weeks and let the wine
develop naturally. In all of this time, no sulphur has been
added.'

While the Chardonnay is looking after itself, the two
more sensitive varieties are kept cold and comparatively
sterile as they are shepherded along the process to the
bottling line. The Riesling is painstakingly filtered and
bottled, retaining the rich flavours and some of the grape
sugar from the vineyard. The Sauvignon Blanc is left for
about six weeks on some of the original fermentation
lees at a low temperature, before being given the protection of bottle and cork at about mid-year.

Ross bottles the Chardonnay when its character has
had sufficient opportunity to develop through contact
with broken skins, yeast, oak barrels and air, and the
malolactic fermentation process has given it a secondary
dimension of flavours. This final step is taken between
October and January.

5

6

Capturing fickle flavour

Buitenverwachting

'Sauvignon Blanc goes through a lot of ups and downs. One day it's beautiful, the next it's heartbreaking. It's very temperamental. Shows one morning and by the next day it's hidden. But the longer you leave it, the smaller the differences become,' says Hermann Kirschbaum, cellarmaster at Buitenverwachting in Constantia.

'About nine months after making, the wine seems to settle, and you finally know what you've got. All the up and down peaks and valleys are sort of mellowed. And after a year-and-a-half to two years of waiting, if the wine is nice and rich, it's beautiful. I really like Sauvignon Blanc.'

Hermann's annual love affair with Sauvignon Blanc starts all over again every February, with the assessing of the vineyards and their grapes' ripeness.

'With Sauvignon Blanc there are two styles,' says

Hermann. 'There's the more grassy style and there's the more tropical, fat, sweeter fruit style. If you want a rich wine, you've got to choose the right vineyard and bring the grapes in really ripe. If you go for the grassy style – and because we have dramatic leaf and shoot growth in Constantia, we find it easy to make this type of Sauvignon – you have to pick it early. Once you have identified the style of wine the vineyard is suited to, you know whether you should pick early or late.'

Hermann makes his eventual decisions after eating thousands of grapes.

'Our vineyard manager and I walk through every vineyard block frequently as the sugar content increases. In the end, we're in there every two days and we eat grapes and talk about possible picking dates till our belts won't fit around our waists.'

1 Important influences on wine quality are the oceans, to the east and west.
2 Hermann Kirschbaum on his way to testing Sauvignon Blanc grapes for ripeness.
3 The homestead, built in 1796, nestles below the Constantiaberg.
4 The vacuum filter in operation.
5 A pumpkin competition helps to enhance community spirit on the farm.

They pay a lot of attention to the weather.

'If we see rain coming and the grapes are ready and tomorrow is Saturday, we will pick all weekend. If you don't, what you were expecting to become a first-grade wine could become a fourth-grader.

'We crush most of our Sauvignon Blanc grapes and allow the skins and juice to soak together, cold in a tank, for at least 12 hours. But sometimes, when you look at the grapes as they arrive at the cellar, you could just squeeze them and drink the juice straight. If I find that we have that kind of lovely flavour in the juice, and less in the skins, we squeeze the whole bunch, uncrushed, in the press and that delicious juice doesn't spend any time soaking with the skins.'

Hermann uses three different yeast strains for his Sauvignon Blanc.

'The one I choose depends on the speed of fermentation I want for that tank of wine,' he says. 'I prefer to ferment at about 15 °C, which is fairly slow and careful, for about three weeks. While most Sauvignon Blanc wines are made to be drunk very fresh, I want to draw the maximum flavour from the yeast and the grape.'

Hermann leaves each tank of wine with a fine bed of settled yeast for nine months before clarification.

'I'm sorry that all the Sauvignon Blanc shows and awards are over before I bottle my Sauvignon Blanc. I would also like to win some prizes. But the long yeast contact is part of this farm's style, so we will continue to wait until Christmas to bring out our Sauvignon Blanc.'

1

Working in miniature

Mulderbosch

'If you have great character in your grapes, you can manage to save that in your wine.'

This sentiment, spoken by Mike Dobrovic of Mulderbosch Vineyards, is a common philosophy among winemakers and can be seen in the practices followed at Mulderbosch, which lies north of Stellenbosch. The two key white wines made in the Mulderbosch cellar are Chardonnay and Sauvignon Blanc, each following a different path, with many deviations between vineyard and bottle.

Mulderbosch is a small winery by South African standards, with less than 30 hectares of its own vineyards, in which both red and white varieties grow. This enables Mike to know each vineyard intimately.

'You can quite easily go through all of the vines, from bud break to harvest, and pick up a feel for what is happening in the season,' he says. 'That determines how I treat every vineyard, when we pick each one, how I work with the grapes and what I try to do with them, and

what I try to do with the fermentation of each tank. We treat every block differently and we are trying to get the utmost out of each one.'

Every block has a selected picking point.

'You can determine your quality point right there,' says Mike.

Sauvignon Blanc has 'hit-you-between-the-eyes' fruit flavour in both skins and juice that tells the winemaker when to pick. These flavours develop to a point and then recede with the unstoppable process of ripening. Whereas Sauvignon Blanc is intolerant and punishes tardiness, Chardonnay is comparatively forgiving.

'The exquisite asparagus and green pepper flavours you could taste in the Sauvignon Blanc grapes may have disappeared forever if you delay picking for two days. With Chardonnay, though, richness may only have changed to succulence after a similar delay.'

Grape skins have to be broken and squeezed in a press to release all their liquid content.

2

1 By Cape standards, Mulderbosch is a small property, with some 27 hectares of vines.
2 Cellarmaster Mike Dobrovic and companion.
3 A young, close-planted bush vineyard.
4 Part of the recent vineyard expansion at Mulderbosch.

'I only want the lovely, soft flavours that I can taste in the skins, so our pressing method, for both varieties, is no harder than the way the old people did it with their feet,' says Mike.

Yeast converts the sugar in the grape juice to alcohol and carbon dioxide at between 12 °C and 30 °C. At the cooler temperature the process can take two to three weeks, while at 30 °C it's all over in a couple of days. Again, Sauvignon Blanc is the sensitive one, and Mike keeps his fermenting must away from oxygen and at a constant temperature.

A small volume of juice made from grapes allowed to ripen longer is fermented at warm temperatures in oak barrels to provide a contrasting flavour in the final blend. Chardonnay is more robust and even benefits from judicious oxygen contact and warm temperatures.

Although Chardonnay grape skins and juice are comparatively neutral in flavour in the vineyard, the familiar rich taste spectrum of this variety is enhanced by exposure to influences that Sauvignon Blanc would find damaging.

Mike explains: 'I ferment Chardonnay in tanks and in barrels. The tank fermentation of rich, sugary juice is allowed to race at 28 °C to give me a fat, creamy, buttery style, while more crisp juice is kept cooler, fermenting longer, making a fresher, more fragrant wine. The Chardonnay juice that is reserved for the barrels ferments at up to 25 °C and has controlled contact with oxygen.'

Mike allows both varieties to gain flavour from prolonged contact with the yeast, regardless of the original sweetness of the juice. Even tank-fermented Sauvignon Blanc spends months of maturation time with the yeast used in fermentation before being clarified. All the Chardonnay remains with the yeast for six to eight months before it is stabilised and bottled.

Bottom of a crater

Paul Cluver

'When, millions of years ago, these Cape folded mountains pushed up sandstone folds on top of the upwelling volcanic granite, an ancient bokkeveld shale plateau subsided in the centre, creating a basin surrounded by a ring of mountains, just like a volcanic crater,' says Paul Cluver, standing on his farm De Rust in Elgin.

'We have a unique climate here because we're isolated from all the other regions. Our vineyards have different altitudes and we have unique weather conditions,' says Paul, indicating the cloud cover that differentiates Elgin summer weather from that of the rest of the Western Cape with its virtually perennial blue skies.

The Elgin-Grabouw region is the only naturally demarcated winemaking region in the Western Cape and shares no boundaries. One has to climb over a mountain ridge to access the valley, regardless of the direction of approach. This hidden valley is east of Cape Town and though its widely undulating floor, at about 400 metres above sea level, is roughly level with many vineyards planted on upper foothills in Stellenbosch, Paarl and Wellington, it clearly has a special climate. Average summer maximum temperatures are far lower than most other South African wine growing regions. This is caused chiefly by the regular formation of thick summer cloud that blankets the valley for days on end, week after week, while the rest of the Cape's grape growers seek respite from endless summer sun. Elgin has an annual average of half an hour less direct sun per day than Stellenbosch, and the difference during the cloud cover period of summer is obviously even greater.

Though most of Elgin's soils are made up of decomposed shale and sand with a layer of clay underneath, there is a lot of diversity in structure, texture and colour. But the dramatic changes in steepness and aspect of slope cause greater difficulty than soil diversity in making the choice of grape variety and vineyard site.

De Rust was purchased by Paul Cluver's grandfather in 1896 and was used in turn as a wild flower resource, an apple orchard and today a commercial vineyard with Elgin's first wine cellar. Though other Grabouw

1 The uneven terrain of De Rust is evident in this
  view of the vineyards in winter.
2 Winemaker Andries Burger and an assistant sampling
  one of the estate's barrel-fermented white wines.
3 An evening performance at the farm's open-air theatre.
4 The estate is owned and run hands-on by the Cluver
  family.
5 Each row has north- and south-facing microclimates.
6 Becoming rare, wicker baskets remain part of the
  Paul Cluver Estate.

and Elgin fruit growers had previously experimented with wine grapes, Paul's cellar was the first oenology project devoted to Elgin wines and was designed and built in collaboration with Günter Brözel, cellarmaster at Nederburg and one of the great names in Cape wine, who, with his viticultural colleague Ernst le Roux, was keen to see the benefits in flavour and style that lower growing and ripening temperatures could give to grapes and wine in the South African context.

Under Günter's supervision, Weisser Riesling and Gewürztraminer vines were planted on De Rust, followed by Pinot Noir, Chardonnay and Sauvignon Blanc. More recently, these 'Eskimo' varieties have been joined by Cabernet Sauvignon and Merlot. One of the new Merlot vineyards demonstrates the uneven floor of the valley with north, south, east and west slopes, all in one comparatively small block.

The pattern of rainfall in the Elgin valley is equally dramatic, with heavier falls nearer to the escarpment on the western side of the valley, and a quick reduction in

moisture as you travel east. De Rust is only 7 kilometres from the village of Grabouw but on average receives half the rainfall. All of De Rust's vineyards are equipped for supplementary irrigation. Though annual rainfall isn't high and summer rain is light, there is a high level of atmospheric humidity in the vineyards throughout summer, necessitating vigilance in disease prevention and providing a further strong contrast with other Cape vineyards.

Though the first Elgin wines are only a few years old, many producers have had experience with the valley's grapes in making wine and a pattern of firm structure and delicacy of flavour appears to be a constant theme. With the ebb and flow that affects most world commodity markets, Elgin's prosperity as an apple producing region seems to have come to an end recently – just as South Africa has started developing a reputation for fine quality wines. This cloudy little valley, high in the mountains, may therefore soon achieve renown in a new field.

1

Individual vineyard values

Neil Ellis

'Just by accident I've become a regional winemaker virtually specialising in single-vineyard wines,' says Neil Ellis of the Neil Ellis brand and cellarmaster at Oude Nektar Winery in the Jonkershoek Valley east of Stellenbosch. Neil makes single-vineyard wines from designated blocks growing hundreds of kilometres apart under widely differing conditions. These are crushed, fermented, matured and packaged at Oude Nektar.

'It all started when I moved from Zevenwacht in the Kuils River district, where I had large vineyards and more than a dozen varieties, to a single Chardonnay vineyard in Devon Valley. I was forced to study everything about that block and make the most of it. Then I moved to Oude Nektar where we did a thorough vineyard study of soil and existing varieties and decided to replant everything. That left me with a cellar and no vineyards, so I went looking for the best and most interesting grapes I could find.

'I've now made wine from just about all of the really interesting parts of Stellenbosch, but what really got things going were two blocks of Sauvignon Blanc – one way up in the mountains in Elgin where the vines grow at 400 metres above sea level, under constant threat of being rained out while it's ripening and another in the Groenekloof ward (sub-region) of the Darling district where the annual rainfall is not even 400 millimetres a year.'

Neil has been allowed to bring these grapes across the Wine of Origin boundaries into Stellenbosch without losing the right to show the vineyard's appellation on the label because there are no wineries within the area of each ward.

2

'I started looking at Elgin grapes in the mid eighties,' says Neil, 'and I was fascinated by the flavours. I made the first batch of wine we labelled as Elgin Sauvignon Blanc in 1990 and made my first Groenekloof wine in 1991.'

Elgin is primarily an apple-growing region on a plateau behind the Hottentots Holland Mountains, east of Stellenbosch, with a unique climate. Whereas Stellenbosch has a classical Mediterranean climate with most rain falling in winter and long periods of clear blue skies in summer, especially during ripening of the grape harvest in January, February and March, Elgin receives significant summer rain and has a fairly regular daily cloud cover shading the vineyards from flowering until ripening. This extends the length of the grape development and ripening season beyond that experienced even in some colder climates.

Though the surface area of Elgin-Grabouw is in the form of a plateau surrounded by peaked ranges, it is slashed by deep winding valleys, creating many microclimates with temperature variations and different wind patterns and strengths.

'The almost daily clouds and ever-present moisture mean that site selection is critical. Like any other region with extremes in conditions, there are places where vines will have a much better chance of ripening than others. We've in fact now removed that Sauvignon Blanc vineyard because of humidity problems and our only current Elgin wine is a Chardonnay. We will plant another Sauvignon Block on a better site.' What happened?

Over 200 kilometres to the north-west of Elgin, alongside the Atlantic Ocean, Neil found a young block

1 Neil Ellis Wines is located in the Jonkershoek
  Mountains on the farm Oude Nektar, which also
  provides some of the cellar's grapes.
2 Neil Ellis, South Africa's pioneer of terroir-
  expressive wines.
3 The operation also sources grapes from
  Whitehall farm in the Elgin valley.
4,5&6 Interior and exterior views of the cellar
  at Oude Nektar.

of Sauvignon Blanc growing in the clay-rich, granitic soils of Darling.

'Here in the Groenekloof, the soil and growing conditions are way beyond our experiences based on Stellenbosch conditions,' says Neil.

'This area receives so little rain, it can't be far from being classified as semi-arid, yet vines love this ground. I have become very involved with this region trying to get to the bottom of the secret. We've dug down into older vineyards to see the structure of the base under the soil and found healthy vine root systems at a depth of three metres. This is unknown elsewhere in the Cape, with the possible exception of Durbanville, but it gives us an idea of how the vine finds water. Our first vintage of Sauvignon Blanc from here was made from a young block grown on a hilly, protected site and though these young vines can't have yet developed a big root system, we had loads of flavour at full ripeness without additional water in the vineyard. The sea must have a big influence. The vines grow on every type of slope here, facing toward the ocean and away from it. When you drive here from the east on a very hot day, the cold air hits you like walking through a plastic curtain into an air-conditioned room.

'We've now invested in this property and are looking forward to seeing the effect this microclimate has on reds.'

Back at Oude Nektar, the planting programme has established vineyards at altitudes over 300 metres. Oude Nektar is located in a narrow, steeply profiled valley, with most vineyards facing south and south-west. The sun rises late in this valley and the vines spend many more hours in the shade than equivalent vineyards a few kilometres away.

'This steep valley creates rainfall. We get about twice as much precipitation as the Stellenbosch average. And I can see these unique conditions have a big influence on the flavours.

'The value of the difference was brought home to me by a scrappy little block of Pinotage. Because it was so small, it was the last in the replanting programme and I had to make its little bit of wine every year. I've never had Pinotage as part of my repertoire, so there was no product to use it in and I sold it off every year. I had noticed that, with minimal vineyard care, it made an interesting wine. When it was time to remove it, we had to decide what to put in its place. I decided to give it one real chance to see what it could do. We cleaned it up, suckered it carefully and pruned it to maximise the flavour. When the dry summer brought some stress, we gave it a bit of irrigation. I gave the fruit plenty of care during fermentation and, because it looked promising, I put all of this Pinotage in new wood. The result was so striking that we've bottled and labelled a single vineyard wine from it and we've planted a new block of Pinotage with the best material in its place. Let's hope the single-vineyard Pinotage series continues.'

Au naturel

Glen Carlou

'The less you do to a wine, the better for the wine,' says Walter Finlayson, one of South Africa's foremost producers of premium Chardonnay. His policy of non-interference with nature has proved to be commercially successful at his Glen Carlou vineyard and cellar south-west of Paarl. A series of full-bodied, barrel-fermented Chardonnays have resulted in many international awards, and has prompted investment in the cellar by Swiss businessman Donald Hess of the Hess Collection Winery in California.

Glen Carlou ranks as one of South Africa's leading barrel-fermented Chardonnay cellars, and this style of wine now accounts for more than two-thirds of the cellar's production. Walter's laid-back style created champion red wines from the vineyards of Blaauwklippen near Stellenbosch at an earlier stage in his career, but now he demonstrates his versatility by harnessing remarkable white wine flavours from Chardonnay vineyards planted on the warmer Paarl slopes.

When Walter and Jill Finlayson bought the Glen

Carlou fruit farm in 1984, it had neither a cellar nor a Chardonnay vineyard. In 1988, when the first vineyard produced a small, unexpected crop, Walter found a spare pair of insulated railway containers, rolling stock and all, and used them to create a temperature-controlled home for all the barrels required for Chardonnay that year. Each one held 40 barrels and the two batches could be fermented at different temperatures.

The Finlaysons' Chardonnay vineyards bear a comparatively small crop of five to six tons of grapes per hectare. They are harvested by hand when fully ripe, starting when the first vines reach 22.5° Balling and continuing helter-skelter until all the grapes are in the cellar, by which time the final loads are riper. All the grapes are placed in 20-kilogram lug-boxes and the bunches are transferred directly into a press for gentle squeezing, without any additives. The resultant grape juice is cooled overnight to allow excess solid matter to settle and be removed, and the liquid is then pumped into barrels. Each barrel is inoculated individually with a yeast culture.

3

4

5

6

Glen Carlou's barrel-fermentation cellar provides for temperature control of the environment, but Walter's son David chooses to ferment most barrels at the natural indoor temperature, between 21°C and 27 °C. Some barrels are encouraged to ferment at a warmer temperature, and others are kept cooler so that they may contribute contrasting flavours for blending.

'Once the rapid fermentation has slowed down sufficiently, we fill the barrels roughly to the maximum, and wait for the fermentation to finish and the malolactic fermentation to follow,' says David. 'We don't want all the barrels to have malolactic. We choose those with the fresh, fruity flavours and keep them cool. We allow approximately half our barrels to develop this secondary fermentation on their own.'

David believes in natural development in the barrel.

'We leave the wines on the original fermentation lees in the barrel all winter. We taste regularly and we develop an evaluation record which is the basis of our blending plan, for when the wines are ready for bottling.'

7

The original fermentation yeast remains in the barrels for six to nine months, depending on the urgency of the bottling date and the rate of development of the wine. The yeast lying at the bottom of one-third of the barrels is stirred once a month. The other barrels are left with wine and yeast undisturbed.

'The barrels themselves are an important ingredient in the winemaking process. We like to use a high proportion of new oak for our Chardonnays,' David explains. 'And I believe in using specialist coopers. I source my Chardonnay barrels from Burgundy coopers.'

Walter and David continue evaluating the wine throughout the fermentation and maceration process until they are ready to begin blending.

'We start tasting in May and try to delay bottling until as late in the year as possible.'

The wines are blended and given a pre-filtration to remove solids, then are made stable in the cellar's chilling tanks before being bottled and labelled ready for sale.

Windy ridge

Vergelegen

'When it's time to start with the Sauvignon Blanc, I become absolutely neurotic,' says André van Rensburg, cellarmaster of Vergelegen, south of Stellenbosch and east of Somerset West. 'This farm is so brilliantly suited to this variety and gives such delicious flavours to the grapes; it dominates the life of everyone around here for weeks. I think I drive my farm manager crazy, tasting the grapes over and over again, block by block. We're always in the vineyard, talking and tasting. We have several Sauvignon Blanc sites on this farm, at high and low altitudes, and at quite varying distances from the sea, so that one vineyard can be fully ripe when another is weeks off.

'It's so easy to decide to pick before you should. The grapes have so many flavours that, after a while, you wonder if you should really wait for more. But we never pick unless we all agree that it's perfectly ripe. It's better to delay a day or two than to pick too early. We have such healthy vines and high acidity that our picking window for this variety, when the flavour is at its maximum, is really quite wide, as long as two or three days.'

Vergelegen, like Boschendal, is owned by Anglo

American Farms, but has had a short history as a premium wine producer, with the oldest vineyards only now reaching the first stages of real maturity. Located on the north-facing slopes of a ridge on an extended foothill of the Hottentots Holland Mountains, high above the Lourensford River valley floor and just a few kilometres from False Bay, Vergelegen has one of the most spectacular and original vineyard and winery sites in the world.

The approach to the cellar from Somerset West winds past the historic Vergelegen Manor House through vineyards and past dams as it ascends to the crest of the ridge, giving views of the amphitheatre of valley surrounded by mountain ranges and the broad blue expanse of the bay.

'What an amazing place,' says André. 'What a privilege to come to work here. I go down to the Manor House about once a week just to spend some time under the camphor trees. There's a tangible feel of history about this farm, and it adds another dimension to the value the terroir gives to the wines.'

Vergelegen became the Cape's great plantation farm

1 Vergelegen's homestead is shaded by 300-year-old camphor trees.
2 André van Rensburg, cellarmaster since 1998.
3 The top of the octagonal cellar is visible against the majestic Hottentots Holland Mountains.
4 The cellar has an observation deck that covers three levels of activity, all below ground.
5 Workers preparing diatomaceous earth for filtration.

under the ownership of Willem Adriaan van der Stel, three centuries ago, with extensive vineyards, orchards and hundreds of slaves. Unfortunately, Van der Stel, Governor of the Cape, was dismissed by the company owners in Holland, his estate seized, his home destroyed and his possessions scattered throughout the colony.

Though most of Vergelegen survived as a single unit of property, Anglo American Farms is the first owner to try to recreate the fame of its founding years. The vineyards are planted along the slopes of the ridge at altitudes of 150 to 300 metres above sea level. The custom-designed cellar is located on one of the highest points on the farm and sunk into the peak of the hill, placing about 90 per cent of the winery below ground level.

Exposed on hilltops below towering mountain ranges and close to the sea, Vergelegen vineyards grow under extreme conditions. The velocity and frequency of the summer winds is the dominant factor influencing every major decision, from vineyard site and composition to harvesting dates. The southerly winds crest over

the Hottentots Holland range like a raging white waterfall and power down onto Vergelegen, sweeping away everything that's not tied down. Depending on the seasonal timing it can take with it most of the vine's early summer flowers, the genesis of the following season's harvest, as well as leaves, stalks, growing canes and even ripening bunches.

'The wind can reduce our crop by 60 per cent,' says André, 'but it can also be a tremendous ally in terms of quality. It reduces our crop naturally and it cools down the vineyard during ripening.'

Vergelegen gained early fame for white wines. The red vineyards have required greater maturity to show special characteristics. André believes that Cabernet Sauvignon and Cabernet Franc will become the most important of the Bordeaux-origin varieties. Though Vergelegen's Merlot earned an early reputation, André believes that this variety will do best as a blending partner for the two Cabernets.

The dilemma of blending

Villiera

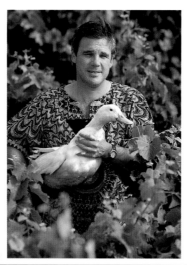

'The three most important areas in trying to make great sparkling wine are choice of variety, pressing and blending. And the most important of them by far is blending.'

This is how Jeff Grier of Villiera sees the major issues in his chosen speciality, bottle-fermented sparkling wine.

'Blending is a decision-making process that allows no turning back. If you get it right, you've got something you like. But if you make a mistake, you can't change a thing. And remember, when you're blending base wines for sparkling wine, you're dealing with complex issues that don't apply to the blending of dry white or red still wines. We blend very young low-alcohol still wines and have to make our choices knowing that this component will have to be re-fermented in the bottle, gain alcohol and millions of bubbles, attain an extra dimension of body and flavour, and further develop over five years or so before anyone tastes the product. That's why skill in blending is the key to all we do.'

Jeff has been making bottle-fermented sparkling wine by the cap classique method since 1984, when Jean-Louis Denois of Cumières in the Champagne region of France spent the harvest in the Villiera cellar. For several years after that, Jean-Louis came to Villiera for the Cape harvest at the beginning of the year and Jeff went to Champagne for the equivalent period later on, before the northern autumn. They also visited California

1 Situated on the extreme edge of vineyard country, Villiera's deep loamy soils adjoin the shallow sandy soils of the Cape Flats.
2 Jeff Grier, Villiera's cellarmaster, and friend.
3 Labelling cap classique bottles.
4 For sparkling wine, uncrushed grapes are squeezed in a press to produce free-run juice.
5 Each of Villiera's mechanised riddlers, or gyropalettes, shakes down the yeast in hundreds of bottles simultaneously.

and Australia together to see how and why grapes ripen differently in different conditions.

Champagne is made from technically under-ripe grapes. The base wine is re-fermented in bottles with additional sugar and yeast, producing a full-bodied wine with higher alcohol content and a natural sparkle from trapped carbon dioxide. In Champagne this process is known as méthode champenoise, and in the Cape it is called cap classique. In the making of his sparkling wine, which is sold under the Tradition label, Jeff's team has to make low-alcohol base wines from grapes that are less than fully ripe. But as grapes develop more quickly at the Cape than they do in Champagne, the strict champagne recipe doesn't work neatly.

'We have to find our own ideal harvesting point for each variety,' Jeff says, 'but with experience, you get a feeling. We taste our grapes many times a week, pre-harvest, and I believe you can almost taste the sparkling wine in the grapes. When it tastes right, we pick. There are four varieties we work with. We have Chardonnay and Pinot Noir, the classic champagne varieties, and we have Chenin Blanc and Pinotage, the varieties we found on the farm when we arrived here. From these we make about 15 different styles of base wine – barrel-fermented, tank-fermented, barrel-matured, malolactic and so on. And these different wines have to be blended together in the right proportion for each of our four products.'

The secondary fermentation process known as malolactic fermentation happens naturally and is a standard feature of champagne. Few Cape producers of cap classique allow it to happen to their bubbly base wines as it diminishes total acidity, a comparatively fragile component in most South African wines. Many of Villiera's base wines, however, are characterised by high acidity and consequently Jeff welcomes malolactic fermentation in about half of those that go into the Tradition blend.

In the making of de luxe products, the policy for the Tradition wines is that they undergo maturation on the yeast in the bottle for up to four years, and maturation on the cork for a further 12 months before they are added to the sales list. An exception is Tradition's non-vintage product, which first makes a market appearance after 18 months of maturation in the bottle, and two or three months of cork maturation.

1

Maintaining control under pressure

Graham Beck Madeba

2

'I believe you have to talk to your barrels individually,' says Pieter Ferreira, cellarmaster in the Graham Beck sparkling wine cellar, 'so I add the yeast solution to every barrel.'

The Graham Beck Madeba cellars, near Robertson, are characterised by carefully worked-out practices, with every stage of the sparkling wine production planned and monitored. Thus, yeast is added to Chardonnay juice in each barrel, instead of to the juice in the tank before it is transferred into barrels, as is standard practice.

Pieter explains: 'We want to gain the most out of this one oxidative stage in sparkling wine production, so we make sure all the fermentation happens in the barrel. We don't want it to start in the tank.'

Madeba's Chardonnay vineyards are all planted in limestone-rich soils, while the Pinot Noir vines have been allocated to alluvial soil with a riverstone base. The Chardonnay for barrel fermentation has been planted in rows that run north to south, designed to provide grapes with the highest acidity levels.

'We used to worry about the noticeable fruit flavours in our Chardonnay grapes when the sugar was still comparatively low. Now we know that this is one of the main things that make our sparkling wines different.'

All the grapes are picked in 20-kilogram lug-boxes, and all the juice is obtained by pressing whole bunches. Following the traditional champagne practice of separating the free-run first juice from the pressed-out second juice, the Madeba cellar ferments these fractions separately. The decision to use any wine made from pressed juice is left to the final evaluation of blend components, before bottling.

Madeba commissions a batch of tiny champagne piece barrels for every vintage.

1 The Graham Beck vineyards share the hot and dry Robertson valley with typical Karoo vegetation.
2 Pieter Ferreira must decide the best point at which to remove the base wine from the barrels.
3 & 4 Bold art and architecture characterise Graham Beck Madeba.
5 Sparkling wine production is very labour intensive, requiring skilled teams.
6 The Graham Beck staff development programme has produced several oenologists.

'We use our champagne piece barrels to ferment selected Chardonnay juice and give it a warm, open, soft flavour to add complexity to our top blends,' says Pieter. 'This is a warm fermentation, with the sugar conversion process running quickly at about 24 °C. The wine only stays in the oak for eight weeks. This is long enough to convert all the sugar and settle most of the solids to provide us with clear young wine.'

The barrels are emptied and the wine is prepared for evaluation along with about 20 other Chardonnay and Pinot Noir base wines, before the final blends are decided. The blends have to be finalised before the important stage of second fermentation in the bottle can begin. The barrel-fermented and tank-fermented wines are brought to the assessment table in March and blend decisions are made before April ends.

When the individual Chardonnay and Pinot Noir wines have been selected for each of the farm's products and blends are ready for combination, a concentrated culture of yeast cells is developed in a base wine solution. This is added to a sugar and wine combination that, in turn, is added to the blend. The newly active, fermenting liquid is poured into the familiar pressure-resistant bottle, where it will stay until it is drunk. The bottles are kept at about 12 °C in a climatically controlled room until the development of the bubble and the yeast-enhanced flavours is considered complete. At Madeba the non-vintage blend of Pinot Noir and Chardonnay is given 24 months of yeast contact in the secondary stage in the bottle, while the cellar's vintage product is given 48 months of ageing. After this extended waiting period, the bottles are riddled mechanically to shake the yeast down into the neck before it is removed by disgorging, sugar is added and the bottles are corked.

Finding the balance

Thelema

'Everything to do with quality is connected with the balance of the vine,' says Gyles Webb of Thelema Mountain Vineyards, just outside Stellenbosch. 'I want to improve the quality of the fruit while increasing the quantity of the crop. I don't believe in the simple concept: the smaller the crop, the better the wine. You need to get your vine growing in balance with your conditions – the soil fertility, the moisture and temperature, and so on – and then you need a serious crop of grapes that the plant is able to ripen fully. There's no such thing as a standard-sized crop. Every vineyard is different, and as a winemaker you're better off spending your time working out what you can do about it than sticking around in the cellar.

'The worst Merlot I ever made was from a tiny crop. I make much richer and more rewarding Merlots from larger crops. In many cases, when a plant is stressed by drought, for instance, a small crop works out very well, but when you're looking at healthy vines, the balance is the thing.'

Thelema's vineyards, sited on the south-east-facing slopes of the Simonsberg, are among the highest in the Stellenbosch area. The blocks of vines are planted at altitudes of between 370 and 550 metres above sea level in soils that are deep, formed from decomposed granite, and strikingly red in colour with significant clay content. They are surprisingly fertile, providing much more vigorous plant growth than most other Stellenbosch farms.

'That's where the difficulties start,' says Gyles. 'I can't learn too much from the other producers in the valley because their problems are different. There weren't any vineyards at Thelema before we bought the place, so we have had to learn everything from scratch.

'You know, winemaking is really a piece of cake,' he maintains. 'There are books about winemaking, but nothing on viticulture that can tell me how to look after any block of vines. Sauvignon Blanc is a perfect example. It's a variety that can't handle stress during ripening. The moment there's pressure on the crop, the flavour disappears. And yet, with our fertile soil and dramatic growth potential, we need to hold back the plant between flowering and berry set so that we don't get excess green growth. Then when the crop is developing and ripening,

3

1. Thelema's vineyards are the scene of constant experimentation in an endeavour to combine quality and quantity.
2. Gyles Webb, the driving force at Thelema.
3. Thelema's vineyards are among the highest in the Stellenbosch area.
4. More than 1 200 barrels are used to mature the produce of 50 hectares.
5. Large plastic containers filled with grapes are hauled by tractor to the cellar.

we have to release the brakes and have as little stress as possible. We treat every row differently. In one, for example, we've removed every second vine to give each plant twice as much space.

'In our farm plan, every Sauvignon Blanc block has an ideal balance of plant material to crop size. We monitor the green growth constantly. You'll find us charging around the vines with our pruning shears, ready to rip off any excess shoots. Once you have the crop in balance and developing healthily, the worst thing you can do is to pick at the wrong time. If we picked Sauvignon Blanc at 21° Balling we'd have lots of acid, no flavour, terrible wine. So we are forced to find ripeness at high sugar levels. I do every kind of analysis of juice, I taste the grapes and I look at the vines a lot. The moment I see some vines looking tired, we take the crop off.'

A small team runs Thelema, with Gyles taking the creative lead all the way from soil preparation to barrel fermentation. His hands-on technique puts him at the forefront of South Africa's quest to make a mark as a New World wine-producer.

4

5

Forty times a day

Kanonkop

Plunge, lift. Plunge, hoist. Push down, heave up. That's the rhythm of life at Kanonkop in February and March. All day and all night.

Looking across the cellar's chessboard of open, rectangular fermenting tanks, the scene is dominated by the continuous punching down of wooden-shafted paddles that are used to break up the coagulated mass of red grape skins floating on top of the fermenting must in each tank. Wielding the paddles are a dozen cellar workers who stand on the sides of the tanks and punch down through the grape skins, mixing the fermenting liquid with the broken skins that instantly rise again to the top.

Each tank is subjected to a complete punching-down about 40 times every 24 hours, until more than two-thirds of the sugar content has been converted into alcohol. Then the rate drops to half-a-dozen times a day, and when fermentation has removed almost all the sugar, the skins and liquid are separated. The skins are squeezed in a mechanical press to obtain the last of the liquid, and the slowly fermenting must is pumped into a closed concrete tank so that the sugar-conversion process can be completed.

But this is not where it all begins. For Beyers Truter, the cellarmaster at Kanonkop, winemaking starts in the vineyard. The first of the creative decisions made by the winemaker for each vintage is choosing the moment when the grapes are fully ripe. Beyers has strong feelings about waiting for this moment.

'There's no such thing as a light-bodied red wine. You have to have balance in a special wine and all the elements have to be in harmony. Picking time is the most crucial period in the making of wine because once you've picked those grapes, that's all you've got to work with. As harvest time approaches, I go into the vineyard a lot, and spend my life eating grapes. When I am sampling Pinotage, or any variety, I chew the berry and spit it out. If the colour is dark, then it's ripe and we pick.'

Not only does Beyers start off the fermentation process in open tanks that, in principle, have remained unchanged for a hundred or so years, but he also selects a high proportion of fruit from old vines for all Kanonkop's top wines.

'When a vine has reached 12 years, you've worked out the size of the leaf canopy needed and the quantity of grapes that each vine should carry. 'You invariably get excellent fruit from these vines.'

He removes the stems from the bunches before crushing and adds sulphur to the grapes to prevent spontaneous malolactic fermentation during the open-tank stage.

'I use a slow-fermenting yeast and try to keep the temperature of the fermenting must to around 30 °C. And then we punch night and day. You can only get the soft tannins and fruit flavours out of the skins during the first two or three days of fermentation, and I want the maximum mixing during this period.'

Comparatively long and wide, the Kanonkop open fermenters create shallow pools of mash, giving maximum contact between juice and skin.

The mash of skins left in the tanks after the must has been removed is pressed hard, regardless of variety, and all this richly tannic must is added to the main volume. Pinotage is generally separated and pressed at an earlier and sweeter stage than the other red varieties, which stay two days longer in the open tanks. However, all the red varieties are moved into the closed tanks to complete the fermentation process separate from the skins.

'We use our closed concrete tanks to finish the fermentation because they have natural insulation and the must cools down only a couple of degrees during the transition. I want the fermentation to finish quickly, and maintaining a warm temperature helps,' says Beyers. 'I also try to have the malolactic process over as quickly as possible, and I induce it in my concrete tanks as soon as the alcoholic fermentation is over.'

All the estate's main red wines are matured in barrels; the complement comprises one-third each of new, second-fill and third-fill barrels.

'Pinotage loves new oak, and I get the best combination of soft tannins and fruit flavours from my new oak barrels.'

The wines chosen for the new oak casks are transferred into them during April and May, when malolactic fermentation is complete. The older barrels are filled in June and July. At Kanonkop, Pinotage spends less time in the barrel than other red varieties. Beyers finds that 'Pinotage has completed the flavour development process, and the fruit and oak components are fully integrated within the first 12 months in the cask. Cabernet and Merlot are kept in wood normally for between 18 months and two years.'

Like most winemakers, he is wary of the effects of clarification. In removing sediment and solid matter, the over-zealous polishing of wines can take out hard-earned flavours. The wines matured in older barrels are in greater need of clarification than those in new oak, and he generally fines them with egg white after between six and nine months. Kanonkop's wines are bottled after blending and final filtration, generally without the addition of any extra acidity.

Although Beyers Truter's ways may be described as 'old style', he is setting benchmark standards in giving his red wines maximum soft tannins and fruit flavour.

1 To obtain maximum colour and soft tannins, the cellar team punches the grape skins down through the cap.
2 Virtually all Kanonkop wine is wood matured, and cellarmaster Beyers Truter keeps a record of each barrel's development.
3 Kanonkop's vineyards, running across the foreground, are on lower mountain slopes.
4 When grown on a bush vine, Pinotage grapes have deeply coloured skins.
5 Kanonkop's open fermenters are wide and shallow.
6 Racking-off red must before pressing the skins.

1 Facing two oceans, the slopes at Saxenburg
  provide a number of different growing and
  ripening conditions.
2 All Saxenburg's red wines are matured in
  the barrel in the farm's functional cellar.
3 Nico van der Merwe punches through the
  cap on a tank of Shiraz.

Picking perfect grapes

Saxenburg

'When I can see that virtually all the red grapes in one of the vineyards have changed colour, the stage we call "veraison", we go into that vineyard and remove any green grapes,' says Nico van der Merwe of Saxenburg. 'If you don't, you get some grapes that are unripe going into the crusher with your carefully tended, fully ripe grapes. We do this separation of levels of ripeness with all our red varieties. There's nothing more important than having only fully, evenly ripe grapes to crush and ferment. If you have a small crop of five or six tons per hectare of grapes like this, you can hardly fail to make marvellous wine.

'I try to have Merlot and Cabernet Sauvignon on cool slopes, and planted in fertile soil. I want fatness on the middle palate for Cabernet Sauvignon and intensity of fruit in the Merlot. But Shiraz is the odd one out. I want my Shiraz growing in less fertile soil, on a warmer site, and I want to see this variety struggle a bit.'

Nico adds: 'Shiraz is the only variety where I deliberately leave part of the crop to get to be almost overripe. The berries' skins will have started to shrivel. These grapes give juice with an extra dimension of flavour. In a cooler season, I look for even more of these wrinkly grapes.

'I prefer to pick all our red grapes in the afternoon if I can. I want these grapes to arrive at the cellar freshly picked and warm from the sun. We don't use sulphur at the crusher and I want to add yeast to the crushed juice and start fermentation as soon as possible. We ferment all our reds at between 30 °C and 32 °C, and that gives us the colour and flavour extraction that has created our style. We use the slow-fermenting South African cultured yeast and that gives us a wine with an alcohol content of around 13% after three or four days at those temperatures.

'We ferment dry on the skins and use all the pressed wine in the main blend. The wine is still warm when it goes into our concrete storage tanks, and it soon starts malolactic fermentation. All our reds are in oak barrels before the end of May, and they stay there for a year. The wines have very little handling or treatment.'

Before being pumped into the barrels, the wines are chilled to about 12 °C so that the solids in them tend to settle. Then they are racked, which is a process of draining the liquid top part of the tank's contents off the thicker material that has settled to the bottom.

'We try to reduce the period that the wine spends between the barrel and the bottle to as little as possible,' says Nico. 'The wine has enhanced its colour and flavours in the barrel and these lovely characters must be protected by bottling as soon as possible. So we give the wines a light egg-white fining and filter before we bottle them. We generally keep our bottled wines for a resting period to settle down before we release them. These reds are generally made available between two and three years after the harvest.'

Heat and light

Morgenhof

The most elusive target in the unending quest to make great red wines is the perfect point of ripeness. Not only does this change from year to year and from one vineyard to another, but the same variety ripens differently under every set of growing conditions. The amount of heat and its daily temperature gradient, the available moisture and the period and intensity of light all affect how and when each bunch of grapes ripens.

'We're trying to get behind the reason for Bordeaux's success with red wines, because we specialise in the same varieties,' says Rianie Strydom, winemaker at Morgenhof, just north of Stellenbosch. 'The best ones have very soft, velvety tannins and this is created in the skins' ripening process by the degree and quantity of heat and light in the vineyards during the months of grape development.

'Some things are the same in Bordeaux as they are here, like our love for Cabernet Franc, Merlot and Cabernet Sauvignon. But our ripening cycle here at the Cape is very different from theirs. We are closer to the equator and have more intense light. Generally it is also much warmer here. And Cabernet Sauvignon and Merlot ripen in their own ways. In Bordeaux, when you kick against the stem of a full, ripe vine, almost half the berries fall to the ground. At that point, the juice in those grapes has enough sugar to make 13% alcohol. If we wait for our grapes to reach this physical point of ripeness, we

could only make port, the wine would be so high in alcohol. So we have to work hard to find the ideal point of ripeness for each variety.' Rianie adds: 'When you can slide the grape skin easily off the flesh, the berry is pretty ripe. When the skin releases lots of red colour into the juice as you're chewing it, you're ready to pick.

'The different varieties have their own requirements. We can create our best opportunities by finding the right piece of land for each variety and modifying the quantity of leaf growth and the size of the crop. Merlot needs the coolest spots on the farm to do best and has a naturally bigger crop than Cabernet Sauvignon. We thin out some of the Merlot bunches early in the season, so we end up with a crop of about six tons per hectare of each variety.'

Both Cabernet Sauvignon and Merlot are fermented at between 25 °C and 30 °C in stainless steel tanks.

'We don't have heaters in our tanks, so if we have cool weather, we compensate by building up a high concentration of yeast in the fermenting must, and the increased yeast activity pushes up the temperature.'

Rianie pumps the liquid from the bottom of the tank to shower over the top of the skins that float on the surface. This mixing cycle ensures that all the juice has the opportunity to gain colour and flavour from the skins.

The closed tanks allow Rianie to leave the skins and

wine together after fermentation with little risk of oxidation. This process, known as maceration, is designed to allow grape tannins, extracted from the skins, to soften in flavour. Once the liquid has been drained out of the fermentation tanks, the small percentage of wine remaining in and between the skins has to be squeezed out in the press.

'I don't want to extract too much tannin from my Merlot,' says Rianie. 'There's a point where the hard flavours begin to dominate. I press Merlot slowly and taste the must often to find the point to stop. In this way, I get only the flavours I want in my wine. Cabernet Sauvignon is easier. I can use more of the pressed must in the final blend and it gives an added richness and mouth feel to the wine.'

All the Cabernet Sauvignon and Merlot wines are matured in small French oak casks in an underground cellar, where the temperature remains about 16 °C all year. The red wines are removed for clarification and bottling after they have spent 18 months to two years in oak.

'I've introduced a new technique called "rack and return" to increase flavour and tannin concentration. When the sugar is about half fermented, I take all of the liquid out of the tank, expose it to oxygen, then pump it back on top of the skins. I might even do this twice, especially to Cabernet Franc, my personal favourite.'

1 In the circular barrel cellar at Morgenhof, the temperature and humidity are maintained at the same level all year.
2 The neatly cultivated vineyards at Morgenhof are terraced up the foothills of the Simonsberg.
3 Morgenhof is one of several cellars on the Stellenbosch wine route that offer alfresco lunches.
4 An ornamental garden is situated above the underground cellar.
5 Rianie Strydom models her wines on the French style.

1

Re-evaluating assets

Boschendal

2

Like a supertanker changing direction, Boschendal wine estate is ploughing through a dramatic change of course. This asset-rich collection of old Cape farms is setting out after new objectives. After 20 years as the favourite white wine brand of South Africa's yuppie generation, Boschendal is redirecting its energies toward the development of notable red wines. Originally a large mixed farm settled by the Huguenot De Villiers brothers in 1694, then a pioneering large-scale fruit plantation developed by Cecil Rhodes and partners, Boschendal's third major development was a frontal assault on Nederburg's pre-eminent position in the South African domestic wine market. During the early 1980s, light-bodied, fruity white wines dominated and this became the focus for Boschendal.

Today, the demand for premium red wines in South Africa's significant export markets and local wine-drinking community has stimulated change in almost every area of Boschendal's business. All resources have been evaluated and, in many cases, modified or completely changed. Some 150 hectares of vineyard were uprooted in a single year and a vast white wine cellar has all but vanished behind an imposing red wine production unit.

Boschendal has discovered a focus as a farming business with dozens of income streams (from pigs to frozen meals) making way for the new single-minded pursuit of great red wines. During Boschendal's white wine heyday, over 400 hectares of vineyards were farmed and these were planted in the ratio of four of white varieties to one of red. The re-evaluation programme showed that most of the warmer sites among the areas with best soils were planted with white varieties, while many of the red vineyards were planted on the high, cool slopes of the Simonsberg, where the grapes failed to ripen fully.

As an example of focused thinking, Boschendal chose to appoint a consultant viticulturist with wine-making training to lead this new development.

'There are huge changes here,' says J. C. Bekker, the viticulturist turned chief winemaker. 'Massive crawler

1 Spread below the spectacular Groot Drakenstein Mountains, Boschendal has one of the most superb settings in the winelands.
2 J. C. Bekker, the cellarmaster at Boschendal since 1996.
3 & 4 All the buildings on the farm have been meticulously restored.
5 The Dutch East India Company seal on a document kept at Boschendal.

3
4
5

tractors have ripped deep into Boschendal's soils mixing lime and other elements to give a happier balance to the soil structure for the vine roots. We're not looking for commercial crop size like the old-time farmers. We want healthy vines that bring the maximum of mineral richness into the wine we make. If we get the flavour intensity I'm looking for, I won't mind if we get only two tons of grapes per hectare.

'We had some very good old vineyards, producing the best wines of the past. We're keeping these, but they are also going through change. We have deep-ripped between rows, pruned the roots and mixed new lime into the acid soils. This will encourage deeper root penetration in an already mature root system.'

Boschendal, flanking the Berg River, has a long history of irrigated vineyards, but the new team has introduced deficit irrigation, which scientifically measures changes in soil moisture levels and allows the vineyard manager to force vines to stress without adequate water when this will encourage flavour concentration in the grapes. The system is designed to add just enough moisture to the vine's roots when it is beneficial to grape and wine quality.

The new red focus is spearheading vineyard planning, which focuses predominantly on Cabernet Sauvignon and Shiraz. 'Shiraz is my pet,' says J. C. Bekker. 'And the most promising vineyard on this farm is Shiraz. It has produced our best wines for the last few years, including one that won our first Veritas Double Gold Medal. We're planting many more Shiraz vineyards on what seem to be our best sites.'

Boschendal's design award-winning red wine cellar is fitted out with closed stainless-steel tanks to allow long and slow tannin extraction. The large temperature-controlled barrel store allows white wine to be cask-fermented and red wine barrel-matured simultaneously at different temperatures in adjoining rooms.

1 The vineyards for Bredell's port grapes are located on the lower slopes of the Helderberg.
2 & 3 Anton Bredell and his staff pump must onto the skins. The intense colour in the skins of Portuguese varieties gives the youthful must a black appearance.
4 The complex of cellar buildings dates from the 1940s.
5 Juice is pumped over the skins and the two are also physically mixed.
6 Bredell port is made from Tinta Barocca, Touriga Naçional and Souzão grapes.

Sleepless nights

Bredell

'Somehow it's always in the middle of the night when a tank of port is ready for fortification, so that night you don't sleep,' says Anton Bredell of J. P. Bredell Wines. 'We do about 20 tanks of port during a harvest, and there's a lot of sleep lost in making sure that the fermentation in each one stops just where you want it to.'

The first stage of port-making is very similar to the traditional Cape technique used to make dry red wine, but the raging fermentation in the intensely tannic, sweet red must has to be stopped with the addition of distilled grape spirit at the point where the wine has its most balanced flavour.

'It's a very slow process,' explains Anton. 'To achieve harmony between the brandy spirit and the fruit and grape tannin, the alcohol has to be added bit by bit.'

Using this technique, the yeast cells are still slowly fermenting sugar even after all the alcohol has been added to the tank. The rate of sugar conversion slows over the next couple of hours until it stops completely. If the brandy spirit is added rapidly, the yeast is shocked into inactivity and the resulting port wine has a hard flavour and is slow to develop to maturity.

Anton Bredell makes port wine from the traditional port varieties, most of which were imported into South Africa by Professors Perold and Theron during the first half of the twentieth century. The first port varieties were planted on the J. P. Bredell farm during 1942, and port-style wines have been made there ever since. The farm, which lies on the eroded lower slopes of the Helderberg, about three kilometres from False Bay, has a mixture of sandy and Helderberg granite soils. The vines are grown without irrigation in order to produce small crops.

4

5

6

Anton's preferred Portuguese varieties, Tinta Barocca and Souzão, have been chosen for the intensity of the tannic content of their skins, rather than for fruit flavours. Their grapes are allowed to ripen until, in the case of Tinta Barocca, the skins begin to wrinkle and the sugar content is between 24° and 26° Balling. The grape juice is very sweet, retaining plenty of acidity. Fermentation takes place in traditional open fermenters, with the grape skin cap being punched down into the fermenting must rapidly and regularly over the first two days to extract the maximum colour and tannin.

'The character of the vintage determines if I'm going to make vintage quality port and which vineyard block will be used for this most special wine,' Anton tells us. 'Though half-a-dozen blocks may have the required sweetness at picking, I have to taste the grapes regularly to find the block with the richness of tannin and juice flavours that will give the flavour and structure we need for vintage quality. I also smell the fermenting must a lot. It's very difficult to taste quality at this early stage, but when I pick up a type of liquorice smell, I know I'm on the right track.'

As the level of sweetness drops to near the point needed for fortification, Anton separates the liquid must from the skins. Brandy spirit is added to lift the total alcohol level to 19 per cent and this causes the rate of fermentation to slow to a halt. The wine is then chilled in a tank to encourage the lees to settle before it is transferred into the used 500-litre barrels in which it will age. Vintage quality port remains untouched in these barrels for two years before being racked off the lees and then bottled without being either clarified or filtered.

Pioneering cool vineyards

Hamilton Russell

'Pinot Noir has shown us year after year that it loves the clay-rich shale soil here, even if it's shallow and not particularly nutritious,' says Kevin Grant, cellarmaster at Hamilton Russell Vineyards, near Hermanus.

'When Tim Hamilton Russell bought this and a nearby property 25 years ago, his ambition was limited only by the quality of the wine he admired and wanted to evaluate. It didn't really matter if it was red or white, or if it was Bordeaux or Burgundy in style, and he planted many experimental blocks to try and find affinity between the climate, the soils and varieties. No one knew then what would ripen properly in this extreme spot alongside the Indian Ocean, scoured by constant wind and with a host of unpromising soils.'

Pinot Noir and Chardonnay headed the short list of varieties that made the grade when decisions about specialisation were made during the early 1980s, and the team set about establishing bigger blocks of these two varieties on varying soil types on the lower-lying and warmer farm, which was eventually chosen to carry the Hamilton Russell banner.

The extremes of climate and the lack of generosity of the soil would only allow ripening of early-season varieties in this Hemel-en-Aarde valley. Pinot Noir and Chardonnay are comfortable under these severe condi-tions, allowing a vine under reasonable degrees of stress to stand in the mild sunlight of March and April, slowly ripening a naturally small burden of grapes. Once this choice had led to commercial vineyards at many different altitudes on the sloping farm, the Hamilton Russell team set out to sharpen cellar skills, emulating the great standard bearers of Pinot Noir technology in Burgundy.

During the following ten years, Hamilton Russell won many awards and commendations for the quality of Pinot Noir and Chardonnay from its unusual site at the southern tip of Africa.

'By 1995, when all of our vineyards had a reasonable degree of maturity, we looked for reasons why some were always producing the wines that were building the farm's reputation and others were generating lesser wines, consistently.

'We learnt some lessons. In general, vineyards love the lower half of the farm and are not happy in the rest. Pinot Noir needs clay content in the soil, more than Chardonnay, and is happier in the warmer sections. And our shallow, broken-shale soil, which was the floor of a shallow lake before volcanic activity lifted and tilted it millions of years ago, cannot support and fully ripen more than five tons of grapes per hectare.

'This made us turn our attention back to the vine-

1 The cellar at Hamilton Russell, until fairly
recently the Cape's most southerly wine farm.
2 Winemaker Kevin Grant tasting Chardonnay
grapes for ripeness.
3 Lug-boxes of grapes are often carried on the
head by Cape farm workers.
4 The underground barrel maturation cellar
includes a private tasting area.
5 Hamilton Russell produces Pinot Noir and
Chardonnay, both of which are barrel matured.

yards. All of the vineyards will now be on the lowest section of the farm, planted in shale, with the Pinot Noir
concentrated on the very lowest altitude portion. The
upper section of the farm, near the ridge that separates
us from Hermanus town and Walker Bay, will be allowed
to go back to nature and grow fynbos.'

Moving some of the Pinot Noir vineyards downhill
has meant extensive replanting. This has allowed the
Hamilton Russell team to increase the planting of different Pinot clones, giving greater tannin content and
increased complexity to the wines.

'The fragility of the environment has forced us to
study our blocks of vines to find the perfect balance for
each one. We only want vines that have a comfortable
balance between the crop of grapes and the canopy
structure of branches, stems and leaves, because this is
the only vine that will give us sweet juice surrounded by
ripe, tender skins. To measure and fully understand this
balance, we weigh grape bunches and count and weigh
the individual grapes per vine every year.

'We also weigh the cut stems and leaves of the same
vines when we prune. When you compare these records
with the wines from each block, you can see how you can
improve.'

Though Hamilton Russell Vineyards now has only

two varieties to harvest, both ripening fairly evenly, the
crop takes over four weeks to bring into the cellar.

'We are often interrupted during harvest by summer
rain,' says Kevin. 'We have to stop and wait for dry
weather, allowing the sugar levels to rise again in the
grapes before we can start to cut bunches.'

Unlike the rest of the Cape growing area, which has
a classical Mediterranean-style wet winter and dry summer, the Walker Bay area gets regular rainfall in summer
from the prevailing south-east wind.

The winemaking process follows a standard pattern.
Kevin uses a high proportion of natural fermentation,
utilising the invisible wild yeast from the vineyard.

Chardonnay is barrel fermented in a temperature
controlled dedicated white wine store. Pinot Noir is
fermented with skins in open fermenters at warm temperatures. When dry, the tanks are closed to protect the
mash. After a short period of maceration, the liquid is
drained off into barrels where malolactic fermentation is
encouraged.

'We look after our wines in wood carefully. You can
go to all sorts of trouble to get the best fruit into the fermenters, and to relax at this stage would be dangerous.
What you have can be made or broken in the barrels.'

1

Rediscovering greatness

Rustenberg

Acclaimed by visitors as one of the most beautiful wine farms on the planet, Rustenberg, north of Stellenbosch, has been established for centuries as one of the gems of the South African wine industry. In 1886, the Cape Colony's Minister of Agriculture, John X. Merriman (who later became Prime Minister), wrote to a friend: 'By jove, I wish I had a few thousands lying idle, or even hundreds. Haupt's place "Rustenberg", the finest place in the district, two hundred thousand vines … sold on Wednesday for £2 400.'

Merriman had his wish fulfilled when his sister Charlotte bought Rustenberg in 1890 and he bought the adjoining farm, Schoongezicht, two years later. Both Rustenberg and Schoongezicht were part of the original Rustenberg 1682 grant, and after a later separation, were reincorporated as one farm by Peter Barlow in 1945.

Rustenberg contains 1 000 hectares in a single valley enclosed by two ridged foothills of the Simonsberg. Generally the land slopes south, facing Stellenbosch and beyond the town to the shores of False Bay.

'We're aiming for the top,' says Simon Barlow,

2

Peter's son and head of the Rustenberg team. 'I see myself as the curator of this wonderful place and we have the chance to aim for the most we can get from everything here.'

Rising in altitude from the valley floor to over 500 metres above sea level, Rustenberg provides vineyards with a range of growing and ripening conditions.

'Our first job is to monitor and try to understand what we have,' says Simon. 'The soil part is easy; we've analysed every block. We've chosen about 120 hectares to provide our fruit. We have forty sites that are completely different, with slopes facing north, south, east and west, plus different altitudes. We want to know how different these sites are, so we've installed computerised temperature monitors in each one. This will give us a much better idea of what we should be growing there and how the vineyard should be handled. We've also installed probes in every hectare of established vines to measure moisture at varying depths in the soil.'

Rustenberg has established a full-scale, scientifically monitored programme designed for fast-track uplift-

3 4

1 The conference room and offices of Rustenberg
   are built above the wood maturation cellar.
2 The cellar's suspended tank fermenters.
3 The tasting room and sales area.
4 The historic Schoongezicht homestead is part
   of the Rustenberg winemaking and administrative
   complex.
5 The vineyards of Rustenberg ascend the lower
   slopes of the Simonsberg.

ment of the farm's vineyards, including a central weather station that measures rainfall and humidity.

'We have established our own nursery away from the commercial vineyards and put up a hothouse in Caledon, among the wheat and barley.

'We've brought in all of the traditional varieties because we don't want to change direction. This farm has always been one of the Cape's top Cabernet producers. We just have to have fully ripe grapes. And because we found that some of the best Cabernet clones were not available here, we've brought them in from France. The planting programme is large scale, with sixty hectares planted in two years.'

With annual rainfall of 900 millimetres, Rustenberg has always had dry-land vineyards, but drip irrigation has been installed in all blocks.

'If we don't need it, we won't use it. But when we do, it'll be there,' says Simon.

Rustenberg has a longer ripening season than most Stellenbosch farms, with long periods between flowering and harvest dates, and delayed harvests. The benefit of shorter periods of direct sun on vineyard and grape development is difficult to measure, but Rustenberg has about 18 hours more twilight each month than neighbours to the south. With most vineyards planted on these shaded sites and concentrating on a small number of red varieties, Rustenberg has planned to avoid the negative effects of a large volume of ripe grapes arriving simultaneously at the cellar. It has capacity at the crusher and enough red fermenters to be able to handle the whole crop at once. 'This allows us to macerate skins as long as we want to on every block on the farm,' says Simon.

Intensifying the handcrafting of vineyards on a large scale has prompted a multi-level skills training programme at Rustenberg. Like most traditional Cape farms, Rustenberg has many vineyard and cellar workers living on the farm and they have tended to become supervisors of the teams of contract workers brought in to do the concentrated activity work of vineyard development and pruning.

'We are concentrating on the development of a powerful team here,' says Simon. 'We involve everyone, improving communications and widening the decision process. In world terms, we're far from the top, so we have to move fast, in a big way, and we can't afford a hit-or-miss approach. But we're putting everything into the job, so there's a feeling of confidence all round.'

5

The African way

Waterford

'We must remember that it is the African sun that makes our wines,' says Kevin Arnold, cellarmaster of Waterford, situated south-west of Stellenbosch. 'The African sun provides the heat that makes things grow, bringing you fortune, and it can take away what it brings just as fast. Its naked glare scorches and dehydrates. It creates a powerful rush of wind over the sea and mountains that blasts everything in its way. Unprotected vines lose leaves, flowers and even bunches and stems under its force.

'At Waterford, we recognise that the African forces are central to our planning of the vineyards and roads, and to shelters like the cellar and homes. We live in a country that has historically had its attention focused on Europe and on the northern hemisphere way of doing things. In South Africa we have seen the French and, before them, the Germans as our role models and mentors in wine. In their colder environments, these wonderful vine-growers and winemakers have concentrated on giving their vines heat and light in smaller spaces. They're looking for tiny crops per vine, so they cut down on the growing area per vine by planting more densely. We have done as much as we can to copy them. In their wet and cool climates they have specialised in Cabernet Sauvignon, Merlot and Pinot Noir. We have followed them with these varieties and trellis the vines on vertically raised, narrow platforms in the European style.

'Some varieties are happy in very hot weather and water shortage conditions, when the soil is drying out in summer. Shiraz is a good example, where the skins continue to ripen, softening out the tannin content even when the vine is showing severe signs of thirst and the grapes start wrinkling. We're going to plant lots of these varieties.'

Kevin plans to establish significant sized vineyards of at least eight red varieties, and encourage experimentation in vine-growing and fruit-shading techniques. 'We need to let the vine grow in the way it appears to be most

happy,' he says. 'We need to give it space, encourage stable and wide leaf coverage to protect the crop from the sun. The balance we choose for each vine should be to the plant's benefit and not just to achieve a commercially profitable crop of grapes.'

Many Cape vineyards are kept clear of vegetation between rows to reduce competition with the vine for moisture. However, the number of dry-land vineyards around Stellenbosch and Paarl is steadily decreasing and the use of controlled irrigation, as at Waterford, allows a more flexible approach.

Kevin plans to encourage more vigorous growth in Waterford's vineyards by selecting certain varieties of rootstock and using irrigation to control the balance between the level of vigour and the maintenance of plant growth between vines. This reduces evaporation from the top layer of soil around the upper roots and maintains a lower temperature around the ripening bunches.

He is designing everything to be as flexible as possible, enabling experimentation and changes in direction. 'How else are we going to make a great leap forward? We have to find the kind of flavour that allows us to get one step ahead, to get in front of the people we're currently following.'

In vineyard design, he is allowing for rapid change in standard procedures if this is required or seen as desirable. 'The one thing we haven't found a way to speed up is the time needed to plant a vineyard all over again and bring it to maturity.'

Flexibility has also been designed into the grape processing procedure and the handling of wine. The Waterford cellar has been designed to handle grape loads arriving in lug-boxes or in lined fruit bins. Grapes can be held in cold storage before crushing and the mash soaked under cold conditions for as long as required. Ferments can be temperature regulated and can proceed with more or less exposure to oxygen, with simple controls.

3

4

1 Reminiscent of Tuscany or the south
  of France, the buildings at Waterford are
  approached through a citrus orchard.
2 Kevin Arnold, cellarmaster.
3 The naturally vigorous growth of these vines
  is controlled by the judicious use of irrigation.
4 Waterford's immaculately kept temperature-
  controlled maturation cellar.

Two chateaux

Meerlust

'I have one chateau in Burgundy and another in Bordeaux,' says Giorgio Dalla Cia, cellarmaster at Meerlust Estate, south of Stellenbosch. 'People ask me how we can specialise in Pinot Noir and Chardonnay, and simultaneously concentrate our effort on making the best of Cabernet Sauvignon and Merlot, on the same farm and in the same cellar. I tell them it's easy, if you understand your farm and have a clear idea of what you're doing with each variety.'

Giorgio has mature vineyards of each of these famous varieties, and has had a generation of experience developing his philosophy of desired style and the technique that needs to be used for each one.

'With Chardonnay, we have set as our benchmark the wines of Meursault. These wines are rich and complex, with lots of emphasis on structure, which gives you outstanding development potential. This may not be the New World flavour of the month, but we don't care about that. We want a classical Chardonnay style that develops slowly out of its initial fermentation phase, gaining complexity and character in the barrel through malolactic fermentation and long contact with the residual yeast in the cask, and finally from development in the bottle.

'If you are lucky enough to predict a fashion and your wine is really successful, you're faced with a major problem that doesn't really have a solution when the fashion changes. That's why we have elected to do the best job we can with the fruit our vineyard produces, following the classical style for each variety. Fortunately we have marvellous examples to follow.'

Meerlust's Chardonnay vineyards are planted on sandy, alluvial soils on the lowest altitude block along-

side the Eerste River. These mature vines grow in lush leaf cover and are able to ripen the crop to high sugar levels.

'I'm looking for a high degree of ripeness,' says Giorgio, 'that I call "over-ripeness" because, in this state, the Chardonnay grapes contain vanillin, which is an essential part of Chardonnay's charm. This vanillin combines wonderfully with the vanilla flavours you get from new oak. We give the juice an overnight soak at a low temperature to reduce its solid content and then all of it goes into barrels.

'We started out fermenting Chardonnay using different barrels, but we've moved through the flavour spectrum and now use only heavy toast. We want as much complexity as possible, and a combination of intensity of flavour and elegance. We want every barrel to have malolactic fermentation and we stir the yeast regularly during the long period of barrel maturation. There's no short-cut to the succulent, sweet flavours of great Chardonnay.'

The Meerlust vineyards are in an extreme position at the southern end of a ridge of Stellenbosch gravel soil, facing into the southerly winds that blow off the ocean. All are within six kilometres of False Bay. These sites have produced top grapes for centuries and have been home to some of Stellenbosch's most highly regarded red varieties.

Meerlust's first owner, Henning Hüsing, became the Cape's richest farmer and, under his control, Meerlust was a bigger grape producer than Simon van der Stel's Constantia estate.

Recent generations of the Myburgh family (owners of Meerlust since 1757) were the first to plant Cabernet

3

4

1　Hannes Myburgh, whose family have owned
　　Meerlust since 1757.
2　Winemaker Giorgio Dalla Cia tasting Chardonnay
　　in the white wine maturation cellar.
3　Stainless steel barrel racks require lots of space,
　　but allow easy access for a forklift.

4　Meerlust's eighteenth-century homestead seen
　　against the jagged peaks of the Helderberg.
5　Best known for its red wines and Chardonnay,
　　the Meerlust vineyards now also include
　　Sauvignon Blanc and Viognier.

Sauvignon and Pinot Noir in the clay-rich gravel soils and establish an important red wine heritage.

'Our oldest Pinot Noir vineyards are in their thirties and you can taste the value of the maturity in the texture and richness of the wine,' says Giorgio. 'The rocks and pebbles contribute to the intensity in the juice. Our job is to maintain the fragrance and freshness through the period of warm fermentation and the maturation programme.

'We like to do the malolactic fermentation in the barrel – again in heavy toasted barrels. This gives the wine more substance, it stabilises the colour of this rather sensitive variety, and you end up with more complex flavours.

'Then we move to the Bordeaux side of the farm, to the Merlot and the Cabernet. Once again we have to do our best to understand what these varieties are all about. We have seen Merlot happier on the more fertile soils and found that Cabernet does extremely well on the stony ground.

'In making our Merlot, we want to emphasise the mineral character. We ferment a little cooler than Pinot Noir and concentrate on getting the softest, ripest tannins from the grape skins. With Cabernet Sauvignon, we start with an even smaller crop. This gives us the powerful central structure that you'll find throughout the process – from juice, through extended maceration on the skins, to the long maturation in new oak. This massive structure is the backbone for our biggest and probably longest lasting wine, our Bordeaux blend, which we call "Rubicon".'

5

White wine tunes

De Wetshof

'Chardonnay is a piano,' says Danie de Wet of De Wetshof in Robertson, the wine centre of the Klein Karoo. 'You can play any tune you like with Chardonnay. You can make full-bodied or racy, elegant wines. If you use different clones, you get contrasting flavours. When you plant Chardonnay in a vineyard with a different soil, the style changes. You can use more or less wood to modify the flavour.

'These are not quality issues but an indication of Chardonnay's extraordinary ability to be flexible. And Robertson's growing conditions are so well suited to Chardonnay that this adaptability is extended and expanded.'

Danie's father, Johann, made white wines from Chenin Blanc and Cape Riesling in the De Wetshof cellar. Faced with a choice of wine universities on leaving school, Danie chose Geisenheim in Germany, because it specialised in white wines. It was here that he learnt about cold fermentation, yeast selection and cellar hygiene.

Returning to Robertson, Danie brought new ideas into conflict with traditional practice and, before long, new equipment was being installed and vineyards of varieties with unfamiliar names were being planted. At first, the chosen direction was German and blocks of Weisser Riesling and Gewürztraminer were established. Then, for the first time, the market took over and Robertson's first Chardonnay and Sauvignon Blanc vineyards were rooted in the arable, level soils alongside the Breede River.

These wines were launched to the South African wine-drinking community in the early eighties at record prices for dry white wines and, for the first time, De Wetshof was a brand name.

'In the beginning, we set out to maximise the area under Chardonnay. We got every stick of the available plant material, took them to a nursery for grafting and planted them on the first available land. When Robertson saw the success of Chardonnay, this process was repeated around the district. Naturally, we made many mistakes, especially here at De Wetshof where we were first. But this has given us a terrific head start in specialisation. We've learnt a lot and incorporated many changes since those days.

'We know that Robertson's growing and ripening conditions suit white wines very well, but we will continue to try to learn a great deal more about De Wetshof and its affinity with our chosen white varieties.

3

1 The different soils on De Wetshof create a variety of wine styles.
2 Danie de Wet pioneered quality white wines in the Breede River valley.
3 The dry conditions in Robertson make irrigation essential.
4 The farm's elegant offices and cellars.
5 A hint of Danie's German training can be seen on this carved barrel.

'Chardonnay is very well suited to this farm. Over the years, we have planted Chardonnay on every soil type and land elevation. We know we get richer, fuller wines on our red Karoo soils and racier, more delicate wines on the chalky soils higher up the slopes. Certain vineyards have shown us that they always produce individual and highly attractive flavours. In the last few years we've set out to find out why this should be, so we can try to make the most of it. These wines are now bottled individually as single-vineyard products.

'Though red wine is very fashionable and profitable, we'll stay focused on whites at De Wetshof. We've planted a bit of red but will concentrate on just three white varieties.

'I'm convinced that Sauvignon Blanc will become the everyday wine of this country and the only contender to Chardonnay for the making of our top wines of the future is Sémillon. This variety is remarkably in tune with the conditions at De Wetshof. It makes wine with a richly textured mouth feel and has a delicious crispness that we think is coming from the limestone.'

Without irrigation, vines will not grow and ripen at De Wetshof. This has brought scientific organisation to the owner's trailblazing style. De Wetshof installed com-

5

puterised irrigation in 1982 and began using neutron probes not long after. Today, De Wetshof's two farms have over 140 neutron probes measuring the available moisture below the plant to a depth of two metres. Measurements are recorded twice a week. Knowledge of the vine's current and anticipated health and stress levels enables the desired balance between the plant and its crop to be managed more effectively.

'We want good leaf and plant growth without excessive vegetation. Then we won't need to use a topping machine on the vines. We can control this balance now by measuring the environment around the vine and giving it just enough moisture, and only when we want to. This enables us to control the size of individual grapes and allows us to even out the performance of a whole vineyard, regardless of natural imbalances such as changes in soil structure and composition from place to place.

'We have a new generation of winemakers making excellent red wines, which is an exciting development, but at De Wetshof we still have lots more to learn about making ever-better white wines.'

1 From Fairview the horizon is dominated by the Simonsberg and the Groot Drakenstein Mountains.
2 Charles Back, the farm's innovative owner.
3 Fairview has also become famous for its wide range of cheeses.
4 Peacocks grace the gardens at Fairview.
5 This novel housing for the goats is in front of the winery.

Market drivers

Fairview

'My father, Cyril, was a passionate farmer. The cellar was only a means to an end for him,' says Charles Back, leader of the Fairview team. 'I'm much more market driven. I can't see the sense in making wines that no one really wants. So it's important that people are excited by the style of wine we're making and then its up to us to make one of the best in the category. Not only do we endeavour to be tops, we also try to be the first.

'It's all about enthusiasm. We want our customers to be excited by what we're making. That's a wonderful feeling and we want to get that feeling more.'

Though Charles takes a high-profile stance in South Africa's export market, he fronts a very effective team at Fairview. Cellarmaster Anthony de Jager and marketing manager Jeremy Borg provide the creative and practical follow-up to Charles's innovative stimulus.

While many South African wineries are re-evaluating past strategies, Fairview is well advanced on a very different course to that inherited by Charles.

'I realised that we had to get the basics right and we had to be brutally honest,' says Charles. 'We used to have a lot of white varieties: Sauvignon Blanc, Sémillon, Chenin Blanc. We couldn't make them give their best here. We knew that red wines get lots of fruit flavour and wonderful colours at Fairview, so we evaluated lots of red varieties as replacements. I'm not convinced that Cabernet Sauvignon and Merlot are mad about Paarl's long, dry summers and constant exposure to direct sun, so we looked toward the Rhône, where the conditions are similar, and planted lots of varieties that show they love the sun.'

The Fairview Rhône variety programme is already

3

4

widespread, with many mature vineyards of Grenache, Mouvèdre and Shiraz. Large plantings of Viognier show that there's also a place for richly flavoured whites.

'I've long seen that there's a terrific demand for warmer, more generous wines. And they are very suited to our slopes that face south-west and west. Our vineyards face the full impact of the sun until it sets over the Atlantic. We aim to get as much fruit flavour as possible, and you only get the maximum rich and appealing flavour when every part of the grape is ripe. When we bring in the crop, we try to crush the grape as little as possible, which means that many whole berries go into the ferment.'

In the construction of the Fairview style, long periods of cold soaking of skins and juice aim to extract early colour before fermentation starts. Many of

5

these fruity red wines are drained off the skins and pumped into barrels before fermentation is complete.

'Because we have some whole berries in the tank fermentation, we often find we have sugar trapped that we can't measure when we analyse the must. By squeezing everything, we extract this sugar and, by fermenting it out in barrel, we get an extra degree of complexity from the wood. I believe in going into oak with red wines as early as possible. The fruit and wood flavours marry, the colour is enhanced, and the wine is rich and approachable earlier.' Fairview's innovative practices have included micro-oxygenation and maturation of red wines on their lees in the barrel.

1 Tipping a 400 kg grape bin by forklift.
2 Harvesting Cabernet Sauvignon grapes.
3 The entrance to the estate.
4 Racking (drawing) red wine from barrels.
5 Owner Norma Ratcliffe.
6 Pinotage vineyard singed by fire in 2000.
7 Winemaker Louis Nel.

Storm in a basin

Warwick

Warwick is surrounded by great Cape wineries on high-value vineyards, and can be seen to be a central jewel among a group of the Cape's 'Grand Cru' vineyards. But there's a storm in the estate cellar and it can be traced to the tiny figure of Norma Ratcliffe.

Arriving on the estate as the bride of Stan Ratcliffe some years ago, Norma brought no knowledge of viticulture or oenology to the new family and concentrated on her roles as mother and wife for the first half of her life at Warwick.

Discovering that the estate's vineyards, like those of the neighbouring farms, were highly valued by winemaking companies, Norma began to agitate for action. And though her technical shortcomings have handicapped her ambitions, she has never shied from her course, taking advice from the best and most fearless of old and new friends.

The first wines were made in a farm shed from grapes held back from a valued customer, following advice from the Cape's unrecognised pioneer of bou-

tique wines, Billy Hofmeyr of Welgemeend in Paarl. The response to these wines was favourable and Norma began to push and expand the envelope enclosing her efforts.

Warwick's shed became a little cellar, old barrels were replaced by new wood, the first Cabernet Sauvignon wines were joined by Pinotage and other varieties hijacked from the vineyards' grape sales business, and critical and commercial success followed. But Norma is relentless.

'I'm replacing the entire old-clone Cabernet Sauvignon with new virus-free material. And in other cases, we find ourselves with too much plant growth in some vineyards,' says Norma. 'The key job at the moment is to get vines that want to grow excess green stems and foliage to switch this energy to the development of the crop.'

Three excessively warm, dry summers prompted the installation of irrigation in the Warwick vineyards. 'There will be many years when we just won't need it,'

6

says Norma. 'But when the need does arise, we'll be prepared. Our vines will never go into unnecessary stress again.' The premature development of high levels of sugar in the grapes, before the red skins have developed sufficient colour and flavour, is a common problem faced by Cape wineries. The Warwick team are working to decrease the size of grapes and bunches, and to boost the number of ripening bunches on the vines.

Finding herself in the middle of red wine aristocracy, Norma the rebel surprised everyone with a champion white. Warwick developed a special reputation for Chardonnay after winning the inaugural tri-nations Chardonnay challenge between New Zealand, Australia and South Africa in 1999.

'Our traditional style has been fruit-driven, with crushed grapes, settled juice, and barrel fermentation with minimum use of malolactic. We have a fairly cool barrel cellar and have used sulphur to retard malolactic fermentation. We haven't wanted a woody style, so we have generally taken the wine out of the barrels very

early. In 1999, when we made this champion wine, the wine came out of the barrels after only four months of maturation. Warwick is best known for its red wines, so we have never had too much fuss made about our Chardonnay. We have always made it the way we like it: fruit-driven.'

'I am convinced that whole-bunch pressing gives better juice,' she says. 'I am also a strong supporter of malolactic fermentation to add complexity to the flavour, so I'll be using it whenever it will improve the wines. And I believe that good French oak adds a great deal to the package, so I will be keen to get the most from cask maturation.'

7

1

Virtual vineyards and winery

Flagstone

There is no sweeping drive through a tree-lined avenue between rolling vineyards to the house and wine cellar at Flagstone. In fact, it's hard to locate the real Flagstone. Whether the winery staff are in the Cape Town docks carrying buckets of fermenting mash, in the Waterfront offices with the all-female administrative team, or out in the geographically widespread vineyards, counting grape bunches and vine leaves with one of the viticulturists, they're always at the heart of Flagstone. While most South African premium wine producers have an imposing home base, Flagstone is a collection of young bustling people operating an assortment of winemaking and transporting equipment, sometimes a hundred kilometres apart, without clearly defined headquarters.

Bruce Jack, founder of Flagstone, is also the central figure in this unconventional business. City-born and educated, child of a musician and an architect, Bruce's

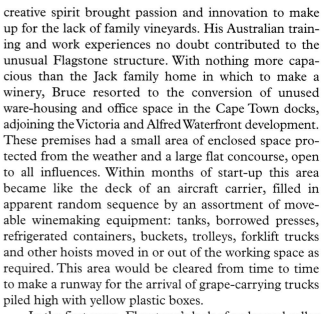

2

creative spirit brought passion and innovation to make up for the lack of family vineyards. His Australian training and work experiences no doubt contributed to the unusual Flagstone structure. With nothing more capacious than the Jack family home in which to make a winery, Bruce resorted to the conversion of unused ware-housing and office space in the Cape Town docks, adjoining the Victoria and Alfred Waterfront development. These premises had a small area of enclosed space protected from the weather and a large flat concourse, open to all influences. Within months of start-up this area became like the deck of an aircraft carrier, filled in apparent random sequence by an assortment of moveable winemaking equipment: tanks, borrowed presses, refrigerated containers, buckets, trolleys, forklift trucks and other hoists moved in or out of the working space as required. This area would be cleared from time to time to make a runway for the arrival of grape-carrying trucks piled high with yellow plastic boxes.

In the first years, Flagstone's lack of a planned cellar

3

1 The dockyard premises of Flagstone, with Table Mountain and Devil's Peak in the background.
2 Bruce Jack (right) and cellar hand Mzwamadoda Matabeni, also known as Errol.
3 Bruce Jack and his father, David, in Flagstone's barrel cellar under the Victoria & Alfred Waterfront. David Jack played a major role in the development of the Waterfront.
4 Open fermentation, punching down red skins is the standard practice at Flagstone, using steel or wooden fermenters.

was less of a handicap than the problem faced in grape sourcing. During the last few years of the twentieth century, South Africa's shortage of premium red grape vineyards became a crisis for wineries relying on purchased grapes. As this coincided with Flagstone's start-up, Bruce had to use a combination of persuasion and innovation to get even small quantities of good grapes for fermentation. So Flagstone began to make many different small batches of wine. When you have Merlot ripening at different times in half a dozen widely separated blocks, you have to make half a dozen different wines, no matter how small the volume.

Working with vineyards as distant from one another as Constantia and Riebeek and Elim placed another burden on the fledgling enterprise. Flagstone has a roaming viticulturist who has to guide growers, previously unused to working with perfectionists in vineyard and grape care. Bruce tries to make wine without mechanical handling, so Flagstone also has a high proportion of cellar workers. Pushing presses, stomping grapes, hoisting

4

buckets: there are people bustling around Flagstone, day and night, most weeks of the year. The fermentation season lasts much longer at Flagstone as cold rooms are used to chill grapes, and grape mash can be held near to freezing for many weeks for maximum colour extraction.

Such a decentralised business, involving the personalised creative input of dozens of people, requires a dedicated team, strongly motivated and regularly in touch with one another.

Bruce's vision and communication skills, supported by the intense camaraderie of the multilingual team of young workers at Flagstone, have quickly created a dynamic business that follows no precedent or equivalent.

Flagstone's customers, few of whom have seen one of Flagstone's contracted vineyards or visited the winery, have a strong idea of the passion and idealism of the business, gained from Bruce's continuous stream of breezy newsletters and the company's branded website, where this disparate business comes effectively together.

Multi-layered innovation

West Coast Organics

A highly original wine producer has appeared, virtually ready-made, in the Vredendal area. In the semi-arid upper West Coast, private-cellar wine producers are hard to find. Though the Olifants River area around Vredendal is South Africa's second largest producer of wine, sourced from the ribbon of vineyards decorating the river on its sweep from mountains to the sea, almost all of this wine is made in five industrial-sized co-operative cellars.

The imposing steelwork, the suspended tanks, the cavernous cold rooms and the towering crane of the new, private Rossouw family winery at Trawal are indicators of a very different approach to large-scale winemaking.

West Coast Organics is a private company, owned by the Rossouw family and four grape-growing farms in Trawal, Vredendal and Van Rhynsdorp. Red variety vines are grown under organic disciplines in the three neighbouring districts. Juice from this fruit is fermented at the Rossouw winery in small batches under laboratory-

standard conditions to produce intensely flavoured red wines.

Most significant new businesses start with a difference: West Coast Organics has jump-started into life with a whole stream of original goals and techniques. The first organically grown wine grapes on the West Coast were planted in 1997 by Willem Rossouw in Van Rhynsdorp in the aftermath of a catastrophic storm that destroyed a table grape farm. The saline soils of this semi-desert area hamper most forms of crop production. The only supplementary irrigation available is water from highly salted boreholes, which has to be supplied constantly to plants growing in the equally salty ground. The consequent lack of vigour and restrained crop volumes resulting from the salt, which normally would be a severe handicap, proved to be of value in the production of quality red wines. Even the grape berry sizes are smaller than the average and this enhances the colour in red wine. The whole area has very low daily humidity levels,

1 Gravity-flow winemaking requires suspended tanks.
2 The crane enables grape bins and even tanks to be hoisted to eliminate pumping.
3 Van Rhynsdorp's arid vineyards have highly saline soils, reducing vigour.
4 The mobile press can be positioned under any tank.
5 Dudley Wilson, West Coast Organics' winemaker.

3

4

5

making large-scale organic farming simple and practical.

The Rossouw winery shares premises with the family's table grape packing and storage business. Conveniently, this operation ships out the last cases of export table fruit before the first red wine grapes are ready for harvest, allowing full use of the large cooling plant, cool rooms and other infrastructure for wine-making. One of the Rossouw brothers has a nearby steel engineering business, so the fledgling winery has had tanks, platforms, bins and hoists made on the spot, as required.

In pursuit of maximum flavour concentration and the extraction of soft tannins, Dudley Wilson, West Coast Organics winemaker, has planned cellar operations that avoid pumping grapes, skins and mash. These are instead hoisted above receiving bins or tanks and dropped into place by gravity. Large quantities of grapes can be harvested in boxes or bins, transported uncrushed, and then sorted by teams of expert grape

handlers under temperature controlled conditions. The grapes are then cooled to 0 °C before crushing and the mash is cold soaked. Even when many vineyards ripen simultaneously, the different blocks of mash can be separated and kept at 0 °C for months if necessary while awaiting fermentation. This permits gentle colour and tannin extraction before fermentation commences, and also allows the controlled start of fermentation, which prevents bottlenecks at the press.

The Rossouw winery is a significantly large red wine cellar, positioned like an island in the middle of Trawal's white vineyards, employing revolutionary methods to retain red grape flavours.

The first vintage of 700 tons in 2002 will be boosted by extensive red variety plantations, organically farmed, on all four shareholder properties. The winery is planned and equipped to extend these techniques to 2 000 tons of red grapes.

DESSERT AND FORTIFIED WINES

Most of the world's wines are sold with a certain degree of sweetness that is either retained in the juice during fermentation or added to it afterwards. This fractional amount of sugar is often masked by the natural acidity in the grapes. In a special category are wines with pronounced sweetness, and these range from handcrafted classics made from the fermented juice of over-mature, sugar-saturated fruit – some of which are fortified with additional alcohol – to unfermented grape juice that is preserved with alcohol. The latter is a curiosity that can barely be called a wine, as it has not undergone the fermentation process, but it is generally grouped with other fortified wine products.

In the making of dessert wines, the yeast modifying the sugar in the grape juice during the fermentation process is stopped in its tracks when the ambient temperature of the liquid drops below 10 °C or, in the case of fortified wines, when the alcohol in the liquid reaches

more than 15 per cent of the total. When the yeast is removed, the wine that results has the flavour of what is left of the original grape juice.

In the Cape there are two important dessert wine styles that, made without fortification, contain alcohol derived only from the yeast fermentation of the grape juice. One of these is Special Late Harvest, which is made from very ripe grapes that have benefited from the dehydrating and flavour-enhancing fruit fungus *Botrytis cinerea*. By regulation, it must contain between 30 and 50 grams of sugar per litre. The second, Noble Late Harvest, is produced from even riper grapes that have been shrunken by *Botrytis cinerea* and contain about one-third sugar. Once again, all the alcohol is derived from the yeast fermentation.

Botrytis cinerea is a fungus that settles in the grape skin and allows moisture to evaporate without permitting any other organism or material to penetrate. The

1 In a cellar using the solera system, the final blend of sherry is drawn from the barrels in the lowest level containing the oldest wine.
2 Muscat d'Alexandrie, or hanepoot, is a variety used for many fortified sweet wines in South Africa.
3 Vin de Constance, a recreation of the legendary Constantia wine of previous centuries.
4, 5 & 6 Some of the country's finest dessert wines are made from botrytised grapes.
7 Nederburg has produced a range of quality dessert wines for many decades.
8 & 9 Lowell Jooste of Klein Constantia tastes Muscat de Frontignan grapes, which are allowed to become ultra-ripe before being picked for the estate's celebrated Vin de Constance.

flavour in the grape juice is thus concentrated, and the grape gains sweetness without losing acidity. Whenever a grape grower notices the fungus in the vineyard, either the harvesting team will be instructed to pick quickly before the infection can spread or, if there is the intention to make a Special or Noble Late Harvest wine, the outbreak will be allowed to develop. A 48-hour period of high humidity when the grapes are at just the right level of ripeness provides ideal conditions for the fungus to spread rapidly, reducing a yield of ten tons to five or even three. Proximity of the vineyard to the sea is an advantage as it ensures the humidity required.

The fungus affects only some of the grapes in a bunch, so the wine is made from a percentage of normally over-ripe grapes and some blackened, wizened ones. In the making of Noble Late Harvest, bunches are harvested by hand and, at the cellar, they are squeezed slowly and gently. The juice is chilled to around 5 °C, stay-

ing at that temperature for several days so that as much solid matter as possible settles to the bottom of the tank.

Fermentation then begins and, as it occurs in the cooler weather at the end of summer, can take a long time, even months to complete, generally leaving considerable unfermented sugar. Some winemakers like to ferment part of the wine in barrels, achieving flavours that complement those gained in the tank. The yeast continues to convert sugar until it has produced the required balance of alcohol and sugar. The wine then generally stays in oak or tank for seven to eleven months before being clarified and bottled.

Sherries and port-style wines are fortified with additional alcohol in the same style as the European originals. Variations include South African specialities such as Hanepoot (made from Muscat d'Alexandrie grapes) and white and red muscadels.

✻

6

The Cape Winelands

The Cape winelands have much to offer the traveller: secluded valleys surrounded by towering mountain crags, historic towns and gracious homesteads set among the vineyards and, not least, the opportunity to sample hundreds of different wines on the farms where they were grown. Most of the region's wine farms are now open for tastings and many provide lunches, enabling guests to try local cuisine in combination with the local wines. Cape wines are becoming known and appreciated throughout the world, but there can be no doubt that the best place to enjoy them is under the sun, among the mountains and people that nurtured them.

Left: A picnic on the lawns at Boschendal is a highlight of a visit to the Cape winelands.

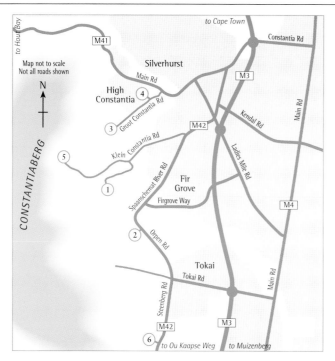

1 BUTENVERWACHTING   4 HIGH CONSTANTIA
2 CONSTANTIA UITSIG   5 KLEIN CONSTANTIA
3 GROOT CONSTANTIA   6 STEENBERG

Constantia

Developing Van der Stel's heritage

'This piece of land was once part of Simon van der Stel's illustrious Constantia wine farm,' says Herman Hane-kom, manager of the Steenberg wine estate in Tokai. 'But here he grazed sheep in the veld. We are many kilometres south of Groot Constantia where the great vineyards of three centuries ago were planted, and though these two farms are in the same wine of origin area, they are different in many ways. We have much more wind in Tokai and when we laid out our first Steenberg vineyards, I had to plan how these should face the impact of wind for every variety, for every level up the mountainside and for changes in the soil from place to place.'

Formerly Boschendal's viticulturist, Herman was employed to plan Steenberg, developing a premium wine producer from scratch in South Africa's prestigious Constantia Valley, on land where previously orchards and natural vegetation grew.

'We did a detailed soil study with over 3 000 holes in a grid across the farm, and drew a geological map that shows us what is under each hectare. Then I came here to soak up the atmosphere and absorb the effect of what seemed to be the major influences. I spent hours sitting among the natural vegetation on slopes, in the hollows, behind the rows of old pine trees, on the windiest days and in the heat of summer. Though we could study the records of the traditional vineyard growing part of

Constantia, we were starting with a blank sheet here.'

Herman's work at Steenberg started in 1990 and he has since observed many of the key influences on vine growing and wine quality in various parts of Constantia, whose wine-producing farms have incorporated this into the growing bank of knowledge about the area. Constantia has 500 hectares of wine-producing vine-yards on these properties, surrounded by and inter-spersed with some of Cape Town's affluent residential suburbs.

These vineyards spread along the east-facing slopes of the Constantiaberg and Vlakkenberg ranges, and into the valley floor to the east towards False Bay.

The mountain chain runs like a north-south spine along the narrow Cape Peninsula separating the cold Atlantic waters from False Bay and its warmer Indian Ocean influence. The development of the ripening grapes in all of the vineyards is modified by the winds, fluctuating temperatures and moisture generated by the proximity of these water masses.

'The weather patterns change a lot, depending on where you are in the valley,' says André Badenhorst, until recently manager of Constantia Uitsig. 'Though the soils vary from the mountain slopes to the fairly level land at Constantia Uitsig, they are mostly derived from granite, have a lot of clay and are fertile. Rainfall is higher in the

1 Steenberg in Tokai is Constantia's most
  southerly estate.
2 Cape farm workers come from many cultures.
3 The Constantia valley is situated on a narrow
  neck of land between the Atlantic and Indian
  Oceans, its vines cooled by sea breezes.
4 Historic wine vats in Groot Constantia's new
  cellar.
5 At Constantia Uitsig the grapes sometimes
  ripen four weeks in advance of those in the
  more northerly Constantia vineyards.

northern vineyards, especially those close to the steep mountain slopes. And the southerly winds are more powerful at Steenberg than elswhere in the valley.'

Grapes ripen much earlier at the southern end of the valley, with Steenberg some two weeks earlier and Constantia Uitsig sometimes four weeks in advance. These dramatic differences happen over distances of five to ten kilometres and at only small variations in altitude. Moving up the mountain slopes, there are even greater changes in vineyard ripening behaviour.

Groot Constantia, Buitenverwachting, Klein Constantia and Steenberg all have high altitude vineyards with high rainfall and cooler temperatures. These vineyards often have difficulty in fully ripening late-maturing varieties and are clearly better suited to certain white cultivars. Reds are generally planted lower down on the Constantia farms especially on land that has any north-facing exposure.

'We have problems with excessive humidity here and need as much sun as we can get,' says André Badenhorst. 'It makes red winemaking quite a trial.' With its verdant vineyards decorating mountain foothills, parallel to the beaches of False Bay, surrounded by parkland and tree-lined avenues, a visit to the Constantia Valley has become a featured part of the Cape's growing tourist industry.

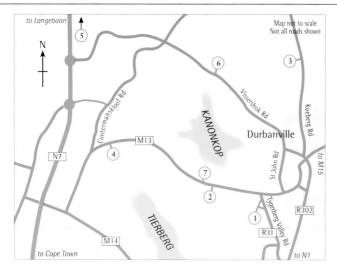

1 ALTYDGEDACHT   5 HAVANA HILLS
2 BLOEMENDAL   6 MEERENDAL
3 DIEMERSDAL   7 NITIDA
4 DURBANVILLE HILLS

Durbanville

Suburban vineyards

Durbanville's vineyards, many of which rank among the most highly regarded in the Cape, are seldom seen by the travelling wine consumer and tourist, though they are just 20 minutes drive from Cape Town's city centre and have a large proportion of Cape Town's residents as neighbours.

Like Stellenbosch, the Dutch East India Company established the Durbanville region at the beginning of the eighteenth century as a production area for wheat, wine, meat and vegetables, to supply ships plying the route between Europe and today's Indonesia and India. Unlike Stellenbosch and Paarl, where the winemaking and trading businesses Stellenbosch Farmers' Winery and the KWV focused neighbouring farms' attention on the supply of grapes for wine, Durbanville was chiefly influenced by the demand for meat, milk and bread in the growing city. Wheat and dairy thus provided a large part of the income of many Durbanville farms.

During the first two and a half centuries of Durbanville's mixed farming history, grapes were crushed and wine fermented in the farm cellars. No grapes were sold. The wines were sold to Cape Town wholesaling companies who blended and sold their products to both world and domestic markets.

The Barbera grape variety has been grown on Altydgedacht farm for several generations. Barbera wine was sold to Cape Town's Italian families, such as the Costas and the Monis, and to Greek families who pre-ferred it with added resin. Other varieties grown (and recorded in Durbanville family diaries) include Chenin Blanc, Sémillon, Cinsaut and Muscat d'Alexandrie, all of which were known by local names.

When Jean Parker of Altydgedacht arrived in Durbanville in the late 1940s, Cabernet Sauvignon, Shiraz and Pinotage were being added to Durbanville's red wine supply. Meerendal was one of the first farms to experiment with Pinotage and Shiraz and pioneered several red wine developments for Professor Perold and, later, the KWV. The first forms of trellising vines dates from this era and, today, wires and poles support most Durbanville vineyards.

As the historically tiny domestic market for dry table wines began to grow in the second half of the twentieth century, the quality of wines made from Durbanville grapes drew increasing attention to the area and land use began to change towards greater plantings of vineyards. From the 1950s, wine has played an increasingly important part in the lives of Durbanville farmers. Some have converted almost wholly to specialist grape growing, producing premium grapes for the bigger Stellenbosch and Paarl marketing companies to crush and ferment.

With large areas of good vineyard soil where wheat once swayed, grape growers have been able to multiply their vineyard holdings. Surrounded on three sides by Cape Town suburbs, Durbanville has a number of agri-

1 Durbanville's vineyards enjoy the cooling influence of both False Bay and the Atlantic Ocean.
2 Jean Parker of Altydgedacht.
3 Durbanville Hills winery.
4 Punching the cap at Nitida.
5 The tasting room at Altydgedacht.

cultural blessings that may keep residential development from swallowing the last vineyards.

Like some of the other grape-growing areas near the west coast, Darling and northern Malmesbury, Durbanville has soils that hold moisture efficiently. Without access to a river, irrigation is uncommon, but fortunately the reasonable volume of rainfall (500 millimetres per annum) and the moisture locked into the clay content of the area's extremely deep soils enable vines to grow and ripen grapes with ease, into the driest summer.

Close to two oceans, Durbanville vineyards benefit from maritime influences throughout the growing and ripening stages. With mist blowing in from the Atlantic during late stages of ripening and south-east winds blowing directly off False Bay reducing summer night-time temperatures, Durbanville has one of the Cape's slowest ripening rates. Varieties ripen at least two weeks later than the average in Stellenbosch. Most Durbanville vineyards also have an early sunset and long twilight when the sun falls behind the Tygerberg Hills.

'One of the most important developments on our farms has been the change to the system of labour,' says Jean Parker. 'We used to have permanent homes for about 15 families on Altydgedacht, and everybody had a job of some kind. Now we provide jobs for town-dwelling workers in the normal way and we bring in contract teams to do intensive work like planting, pruning and harvesting when needed.'

3

4

5

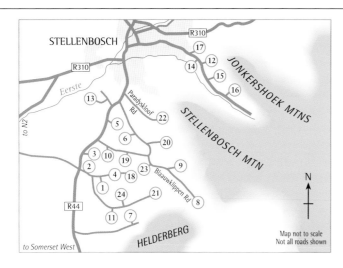

STELLENBOSCH

1	ALTO
2	ANNANDALE
3	AUDACIA
4	BILTON
5	BLAAUWKLIPPEN
6	BLUE CREEK
7	CLOS DU CIEL
8	DE TRAFFORD
9	DORNIER
10	GRACELAND
11	HELDERKRUIN
12	KLEIN GUSTROUW
13	KLEINE ZALZE
14	LANZERAC
15	LE RICHE
16	NEIL ELLIS
17	ROZENDAL
18	RUST EN VREDE
19	STELLENZICHT
20	TALANA HILL
21	UVA MIRA
22	VRIESENHOF
23	WATERFORD
24	WEBERSBURG

1 Jannie Engelbrecht of Rust en Vrede.
2 Irrigation using overhead sprinklers.
3 Guinea fowl foraging in the vineyards at Lanzerac.
4 Jan 'Boland' Coetzee of Vriesenhof.
5 The vineyards and hotel complex at Lanzerac.
6 Chris McDonald of Klein Gustrouw.

Stellenbosch Mountain

Slopes and wind

'Wine is a mirror of its environment,' says Jan Coetzee of Vriesenhof, south of Stellenbosch, on the slopes of Stellenbosch Mountain. 'You get a varied batch of wines from around here because of the mountains and all of the different landforms where they grow the vines.'

Stellenbosch Mountain juts out between the Helderberg and Drakenstein Mountains. Most of the area's vineyards are planted on the south- and west-facing slopes of the foothills, which rise in steps from the valleys of the Blaauwklip and Eerste rivers.

'All of the finer soils are made from particles washed down from the peaks and you'll find more of this mother material on the level hilltops. On the southern slopes, the soils are deep with lots of clay content. The vineyards growing here have less need of irrigation than those on the stony and sandy soils.'

The wide variations in style found in wines made from Stellenbosch Mountain vineyards can also be attributed to the angle of the sun on the slopes, the altitude and the force of the summer winds.

'The mountains influence everything,' says Jan. 'At

eleven o'clock in the morning, the air pushing against the mountain is already rising. Some people are very protected from the strongest winds by the bulk of the mountain. This might make for easier farming but certain vineyards growing in the face of the most powerful winds are making outstanding wines.'

These summer winds normally come around the mountain from the south-east or the south-west and they probably have the greatest influence of all, reducing crops, lowering temperatures and refreshing the air among the vines. Though Cape growers have a concerted programme to reduce the quantity and intensity of sprays and chemical treatments in all vineyards the natural ventilation provided by the southerly winds reduces the need to spray. Altitude affects Cape vineyards in a way not generally found elsewhere, as most of the world's best vineyard sites are comparatively level, with gently sloping soils.

'We have a unique problem with Chardonnay,' says Jan. 'It's a variety suited to many flavour influences. You can pick the grapes at different levels of ripeness and

5

make different wines. If we could grow Chardonnay successfully at high altitudes we would be able to add a crisper, livelier style to the collection. But high altitude has a unique effect on Chardonnay. We get staggered flowering and every bunch grown at 400 metres or higher will have some buds that are weeks later than others alongside them. That's why the Chardonnay vineyards are never the highest ones. Merlot, Pinotage and Sauvignon Blanc are fertile enough to grow at almost any altitude.'

Though Stellenbosch Mountain catches the rain clouds and rainfall is higher than that of the Stellenbosch region in general, most of the leading farmers are installing or extending irrigation in vineyards.

'I lean toward the principles of overhead irrigation with sprinklers spraying water over the leaves and stems,' says Jan. 'Most people are installing drip irrigation, but I feel that the plant needs to receive water in the most normal way and the replication of rain feels right for me.'

South Africa is in the middle of a major vineyard-planting programme but is encountering a handicap not

seen elsewhere to the same degree. Among the myriad plant diseases faced by commercial grape farmers, the incidence of plant virus has a significant negative impact on the plant's capacity to achieve the winemaker's desired level of ripeness in grapes. While the industry authorities encourage the commercial planting of vines raised in an uninfected environment, Jan Coetzee is attempting to identify and isolate individual vines showing no visible signs of virus though they are growing in a clearly infested environment.

'We take cuttings from these vines, graft them and are developing vineyards with virus-resistant, rather than virus-free material. I believe we should be doing the same with vines that can clearly be seen to be more wind resistant on our wind-exposed slopes.'

Stellenbosch Mountain vineyards are flanked by suburban growth and, in time, this is likely to be a threat to the continued development of the many outstanding vineyard sites on the mountain slopes.

6

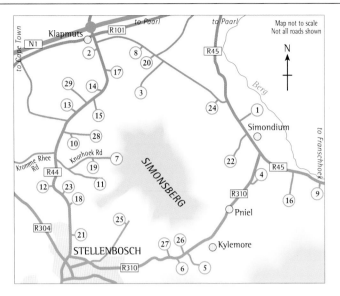

1 ASHWOOD
2 AVONDVREDE
3 BACKSBERG
4 BOSCHENDAL
5 CAMBERLEY
6 DELAIRE
7 DELHEIM
8 GLEN CARLOU
9 GRAHAM BECK COASTAL
10 KANONKOP
11 KNORHOEK
12 L'AVENIR
13 LAIBACH
14 LE BONHEUR
15 LIEVLAND
16 L'ORMARINS
17 MONT DESTIN
18 MORGENHOF
19 MURATIE
20 NIEL JOUBERT
21 NIETVOORBIJ
22 PLAISIR DE MERLE
23 REMHOOGTE
24 RUPERT & ROTHSCHILD
25 RUSTENBERG
26 THELEMA
27 TOKARA
28 UITKYK
29 WARWICK

1 & 2 Stained glass in the tasting room at Muratie.
3 The tasting room and sales area at Delheim.
4 Uitkyk's Cape Georgian homestead.
5 Farms in the western foothills of the Simonsberg.
6 Entrance to the cellar at Lievland.

Simonsberg

Surrounded by vineyards

Most Cape mountains are links in folded ranges or segments of an uplifted plateau. The Simonsberg draws attention from all directions, standing out as an isolated spur in the Hottentots Holland group. Like many others, it is a jagged chain of peaks, but Simonsberg uniquely stands isolated like an island sentinel between Paarl Valley and the broad spaces linking Stellenbosch and Cape Town.

Standing vertically like a knife blade, the upper sandstone cliffs of Simonsberg can be seen from all major freeways, all flights arriving at or leaving Cape Town, and is the dominant feature seen on the horizon from Table Mountain.

Though close to the thriving town of Stellenbosch, the Simonsberg is unmarked by suburban development and its foothills are carpeted by vineyards on all sides facing all points of the compass. Most of these foothills contain deep deposits of eroded granitic material, with pockets of shale sprinkled on west-, south- and north-facing slopes. All provide well-drained soils with plenty of moisture retention.

'Even in very dry years, when all of our farm dams are empty in late summer, the vines on the upper, un-irrigated blocks are in a very healthy condition. We never

have to rush picking; we can just wait for the berries to ripen to the degree we want,' says Niel Bester of Plaisir de Merle, on the Paarl Valley side of the mountain.

Some Simonsberg vineyards are in Stellenbosch and the rest in Paarl. The mountain acts as a dividing line between the two areas which are generally described as the most valuable group of wine properties in the Cape winelands. Most are renowned for their red wines but a few, such as Thelema in Stellenbosch and Glen Carlou on the opposite side of the Simonsberg in Paarl, are also known to make outstanding whites.

The lower vineyards are planted at altitudes of around 200 metres above sea level, rising a further 400 metres on some farms in a belt surrounding the base of the mountain. Most farms have Sauvignon Blanc on the upper slopes and Chardonnay at lower levels. Red vineyards are planted at all altitudes, with Cabernet Sauvignon the most popular and generally the most successful.

Delheim is one of the most elevated farms with vineyards on the north-west-facing, Stellenbosch side of the mountain, at altitudes ranging from 300 to 400 metres above sea level.

'We used to have both red and white vineyards up

here,' said Philip Costandius when he was Delheim's winemaker. 'When we bought the Vera Cruz farm in the neighbouring area of Muldersvlei, we planted our red vineyards there. In my opinion, most of the high positions on this mountain will remain white vineyard sites.'

The Simonsberg is sufficiently large to create wind channels. Damage to vineyards is mostly an effect of spring and summer winds blowing from the east and south. Delheim and its neighbouring farms are accustomed to the sudden onset of a howling gale, and are often left to count the damage to the leaves, stems and even bunches.

'The biggest problem we have is the wind,' said Philip. 'We have ridges where you can get blown away and pockets of protected vineyard land where there is barely any air movement. You have to know a farm like this very well to know when and how much to spray in every block for summer diseases.'

Delheim's neighbour, Knorhoek, is named after the wind.

'Every seventh year, we donate part of our crop to the environment,' says Hansie van Niekerk of Knorhoek. 'My father used to say that the big man has taken his part. I've seen wind so strong that it tears a three-year-

old Merlot vine out of the ground and wraps it around the trellis wire.'

The Cape southeaster does little damage to vines growing on the south-east-facing slopes of the Simonsberg, in Plaisir de Merle and the upper Boschendal vineyards. It cascades down the Franschhoek valley, and ascends the Simonsberg before dramatically increasing in speed as it falls down the north-west-facing slopes.

'The rapidly dropping southeaster and the proximity of False Bay combine to reduce average ripening temperatures on the Stellenbosch side,' says Ernst le Roux, chief viticulturist at Stellenbosch Farmers' Winery, who has been closely associated with the development of premium vineyards on both sides of the mountain. 'Rainfall is heavier on the higher altitude vineyards on both the Paarl and Stellenbosch sides. The soils are remarkably similar all around this mountain.'

Winemakers in Stellenbosch have a comprehensive plan to develop and manage the Stellenbosch half of Simonsberg as a controlled appellation area with approved varieties, crop volumes and quality levels.

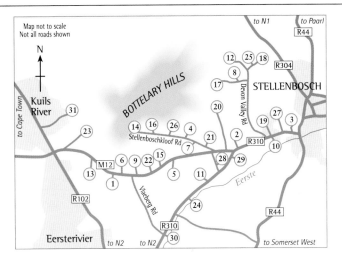

Map not to scale
Not all roads shown

N

1 AMANI
2 ASARA
3 BERGKELDER
4 BONFOI
5 BOSCHKLOOF
6 BOWE JOUBERT
7 CARISBROOKE
8 CLOS MALVERNE
9 DE TOREN
10 DISTELL
11 EERSTERIVIER
12 J. C. LE ROUX
13 JACOBSDAL
14 JORDAN
15 KANU
16 L'EMIGRÉ
17 LOUISVALE
18 MEINERT
19 MIDDELVLEI
20 NEETHLINGSHOF
21 OVERGAAUW
22 REYNEKE
23 SAXENBURG
24 SPIER (SALES)
25 SYLVANVALE
26 UITERWYK
27 VINFRUCO
28 VLOTTENBURG
29 VREDENHEIM
30 WELMOED
31 ZEVENWACHT

2

1 The cellar at Jordan.
2 Jordan's varietal mix includes Chardonnay,
  Sauvignon Blanc, Cabernet Sauvignon, Merlot
  and Pinot Noir.
3 Neethlingshof's 1814 homestead now accom-
  modates a restaurant.
4 Looking over Devon Valley toward Stellenbosch.
5 Distell's extensive cellar complex at Oude Libertas.

1

Stellenbosch Kloof
Polkadraai
Devon Valley

Rich, red soils

About a fifth of all of Stellenbosch's cellars are nestled along the southern slopes of the east-west ridge of the Bottelary Hills, an area known as Stellenbosch Kloof. Although the hills are severely eroded, there is sufficient upwelling of winter winds to create additional rainfall on this leeward side. These conditions, combined with the exposure to summer winds off nearby False Bay, have created an effective environment for the growing of premium wine grapes.

First to notice this were the major traders of South African wines during the twentieth century. Stellenbosch Farmers' Winery were once responsible for the sale of 80 per cent of all of South Africa's wine and – together with Distillers and Gilbeys, also based in nearby Stellenbosch – obtained most of their premium wines in bulk from the farm cellars along the Stellenbosch Kloof. Thus, when consumer interest in specialist wines developed in the 1970s, these small wineries were able to create their own brands with minimal capital investment.

Though the ridge of the Bottelary Hills is a single land mass, there's a significant difference between the

3

soils on the southern side and those on the north. The slice of land along the southern slopes is made up of rich red decomposed granitic loam with a high clay content, whereas the soils over the ridge, facing north, generally have higher sand content and lie over gravel and clay beds.

During the last 50 years of recorded winemaking in this area, the quality of the red wines has stood out, even through an era when less than 10 per cent of South Africa's grape crop went into red wine. This red dominance remains the case today, though there are white exceptions, such as Louisvale's Chardonnay, the J. C. le Roux sparkling wine business, Kanu's Chenin Blanc, and Neethlingshof's luscious sweet wines.

The quality of the whole area has been well demonstrated, with trophy-winning wines coming from Devon Valley, from along the Polkadraai Road, and from the ridge above Kuils River at the western end of the valley. However, future greatness will depend more on the identification of the most valuable sites.

'There's a geological fault running along the north-

4

south line,' says Gary Jordan of Jordan Vineyards at the western end of the slope. 'This gives us different soils on either side of this line and clearly contributes to considerable variation in styles and complexity. Certain varieties have obvious preference for certain sites. We have a block of Merlot we call "Cobblers' Hill", growing on a site surrounded by other red varieties on the crest of the ridge above the cellar, at about 400 metres altitude, and this always produces the most aromatic and intensely flavoured wine among our reds.'

Moving toward Stellenbosch, and at a lower elevation than Cobblers' Hill, the De Waal team at Uiterwyk consistently produce one of the world's great Pinotages in a block they call 'Top of the Hill'. Another remarkable Pinotage comes from a site on the Clos Malverne property on the Devon Valley slopes, closer to Stellenbosch.

These are just a few examples chosen from the profusion of fine reds that come from the sheltered slopes of the Bottelary Hills overlooking False Bay.

5

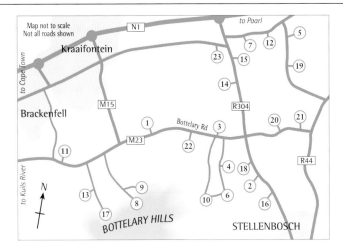

Map not to scale
Not all roads shown

to Paarl
N1
to Cape Town
Kraaifontein
5
7 12
23
15
19
14
M15
R304
Brackenfell
20 21
1 Bottelary Rd 3
M23
22
R44
11
4 18
13 9 2
8 10 6 16
17 BOTTELARY HILLS STELLENBOSCH
N
to Kuils River

1 BELLEVUE
2 BEYERSKLOOF
3 BOUWLAND
4 CLOVELLY
5 DE MEYE
6 DEVON HILL
7 EAGLEVLEI
8 FORT SIMON
9 GOEDE HOOP
10 HARTENBERG
11 HAZENDAL
12 HOOPENBURG
13 KAAPZICHT
14 KLAWERVLEI
15 KOELENHOF
16 LOUISENHOF
17 MOOIPLAAS
18 MULDERBOSCH
19 MULDERSVLEI
20 SIMONSIG
21 SLALEY
22 STELLENDRIFT
23 VILLIERA

Muldersvlei Bottelary

Eroded hill vineyards

Looking east from Cape Town, the horizon contains a continuous ridge of mountains approximately 1 000 metres high, from Hottentots Holland in the south to the Limietberg in the north-east, behind Wellington. In the foreground of this view, the shallow, eroded hills known as Bottelary and Klapmutskop provide the growing sites for a large proportion of the wine grapes produced in Stellenbosch. The area receives less rainfall than the vineyards of the higher mountains to the east, and the extreme north-west slopes of the hills, following the Bottelary Road towards Cape Town, are on the boundary of commercial grape growing, experiencing just enough rain to ripen their crops.

'In this area, it is very difficult to establish a young vineyard, from planting to production in the normal three-year period, without irrigation,' says Ronel Wiid, cellarmaster at Hazendal, Bottelary. The moisture-retention capacity of the soil during the normally dry summer months ranges from excellent in the deep, clay-rich loamy soils to poor in the sand found mostly on the lower slopes, especially in the north-west part of this sub-region, but irrigation is only rarely found.

Viewed from above, the low-lying Bottelary Hills are shaped roughly like the letter J and extend from the suburbs of Stellenbosch directly west to a point about halfway to Cape Town's city centre. Some of Cape Town's eastern suburbs have reached the lower foothills of Bottelary.

Compared with the folded mountain ranges that surround them, the Bottelary Hills are more severely eroded, providing a humped ridge in the centre of the broad basin between Stellenbosch and Cape Town. This erosion has created gentle slopes on all sides of the ridge and these undulations have proved to be well suited to the growing of vines. Vineyards can be found from the bottom of the slopes virtually to the crest of the ridge, along its length on all points of the compass. South Africa's greatest concentration of wineries can be found among these vineyards. Though the hill structure is named Bottelary, the regional name generally applies only to the northern and western slopes. The reverse side is called Stellenbosch Kloof.

One of the key cellars facing north is Kaapzicht. 'The slopes on this side of the ridge are warmer,' says

1 One of several historic buildings at Hazendal.
2 A vineyard worker at Villiera.
3 The vineyards at Kaapzicht are on the western edge of the Bottelary Hills. The sandy Cape Flats beyond are unable to support vines.
4 The Bottelary area has one of the highest concentrations of boutique wineries.

cellarmaster Danie Steytler. 'We find it difficult to make delicate fruity white wines, but everything works wonderfully with reds. They just about make themselves. And that applies to all varieties.' Vines have a lack of vigour on these sand and gravel soils, berries are naturally small and skins develop concentrated colour and flavour. There isn't a lot of summer wind but the lack of fertility in the soil seems to impose enough natural restriction on crop size.

Muldersvlei lies between Bottelary and the conical peak of Klapmutskop to the north-east. In both growing areas, soil types change within vineyard blocks. Most soils are derived from the volcanic upliftment of the hills, with sand and gravel areas and decomposed granite and clay.

Ernst Gouws's farm Hoopenberg in Muldersvlei demonstrates these dramatic variations in soil structure. 'I never realised that on one small farm, all at one altitude, the flavour of the grapes, Merlot or Cabernet, can change so much just as a result of the soil composition and depth. The wind, the rainfall and the temperature are the same all over this property. But the flavour and the intensity of wines made from the same grape, even the same clone, are vividly different from the front part of the farm to the back.' Hoopenberg has shallow, sandy loam soils at its northern edge and shale-derived, deeper red soils with a high proportion of stone to the south, towards Bottelary. Patches of similar red soils abound in the Muldersvlei area and produce rich red wines on many properties.

'It's a pleasure to see and smell the ripe red grapes coming into our cellar from Vera Cruz, our Muldersvlei farm,' said Philip Costandius when he was cellarmaster at Delheim on the Simonsberg. 'The pure fruit flavours are marvellous and the colours are intense. We get grapes that are just like blackcurrant jam.'

Both regions are best suited to red varieties. Although many of Stellenbosch's cellars are located in the folded hills of Bottelary, there are also independent grape growers here who sell grapes to wineries located in other regions that are looking for greater concentration of fruit flavours.

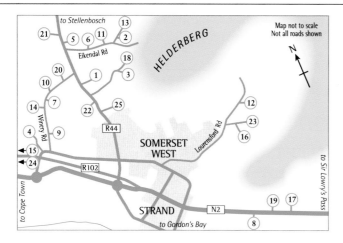

1	AVONTUUR
2	CLOS DE CIEL
3	CORDOBA
4	DELLRUST
5	EIKENDAL
6	GRANGEHURST
7	HELDERBERG
8	INGWE
9	J. P. BREDELL
10	KEN FORRESTER
11	LONGRIDGE
12	LOURENSFORD
13	LUSHOF
14	LYNGROVE
15	MEERLUST
16	MORGENSTER
17	MOUNT ROZIER
18	NOOITGEDACHT
19	ONDERKLOOF
20	POST HOUSE
21	SOMERBOSCH
22	STONEWALL
23	VERGELEGEN
24	VERGENOEGD
25	YONDER HILL

Helderberg

Setting sun vineyards

The jagged mountain peaks of the Helderberg stand like a sentinel island between the valleys of the Lourensford and Eerste rivers, home to the towns of Somerset West and Stellenbosch. Vineyards are planted on land as low in altitude as 30 metres above sea level and ascend the mountain slopes to heights of over 600 metres. Although vineyards surround the mountains on all points of the compass, the majority face west and north, looking towards the sun. As a grape-growing and winemaking region, the Helderberg is broken down into two groups: the area nearest to False Bay, with lower temperatures and clear-cut affinity with Sauvignon Blanc, and the warmer regions further north, with tilted exposure to the afternoon sun that disappears over the Atlantic horizon.

Getting the most from any vineyard site involves maximising the affinity between the growing and ripening conditions and the grape variety. Most Helderberg red vineyards are planted with the three main Bordeaux varieties and generally face west.

'We get lots of direct sun on our vines during ripening – conditions quite different to Bordeaux,' says Chris Keet of Cordoba, a steeply sloping farm with vineyards that slope west, south-west and north. 'We don't achieve anything like the stalk ripeness seen in Bordeaux; when our grape skins are ripe and succulent, we probably still have comparatively green pips and stalks. We have to be extraordinarily gentle in extracting the tannins from our Cabernet and Merlot skins to avoid green flavours. That's the secret to making supple, velvety wines. There's very little haste in the cellar. We have all the flavour and colour we could want coming from the sun and our slope, so the wine nearly makes itself.'

Like most Cape mountains, the Helderberg was created by a granite upliftment of the sandstone and shale ocean floor many millions of years ago. Decomposed granite in the form of clay and various forms of gravel dominate the higher altitude vineyard soils. The easily eroded sandstone provides most of the surface layer on the lower slopes and valley floor. Almost all vineyard sites have a solid clay layer about a metre below the surface.

The gravel soils and, less commonly, some pockets of decomposed shale (as found at Cordoba), are generally heavily mixed with clay, providing moisture-retention during rainless periods.

The Helderberg area has an annual rainfall of between 650 and 800 millimetres, and most of the higher altitude vineyards have traditionally been farmed without irrigation. Today, irrigation for emergency use is being installed on a range of properties.

The prevailing summer southerly winds have varying effects, depending on the degree of shelter provided by the bulk of the mountain. High altitude vineyards like Cordoba and entirely exposed farms like Vergelegen receive the full force of moist air, while Rust en Vrede and Alto rest calmly in warm sunshine on their protected, north-facing slopes. In between, farms such as Stellenzicht have wind-exposed and wind-protected blocks.

'Generally, we have crops that are reduced in volume by southerly spring and summer winds. It seems to suit Shiraz and Pinotage very well, because these varieties have really extravagant skin colour and tannin content,' says Guy Webber of Stellenzicht.

'To make the most of the sun exposure on the ripening grapes and to allow more ventilation in the rows of vines, we're planting our new blocks with more spacing between plants,' says Louis Strydom of Rust en Vrede. Closer to the sea, farmers are planting higher-than-average concentrations of vines.

'There's a move towards a fairly environmentally friendly form of farming, especially around here,' says Chris Keet. 'And it's a matter of understanding the conditions. We get strong winds that clean out warm, stagnant air in the vineyard, and this naturally reduces the chances of fungal diseases. So we have reduced our spraying programme, the recommended doses and frequency from every 14 days to once a month.'

The Helderberg has been carpeted with vineyards for decades, but it has become the busiest construction site in the Cape winelands, with new wineries being erected and equipped on an unprecedented scale.

1 Children returning to the farm community village after school.
2 & 3 Table Bay is visible from Cordoba, on the slopes of the Helderberg.
4 Stonewall takes its name from the traditional low wall that surrounds the buildings.

3

4

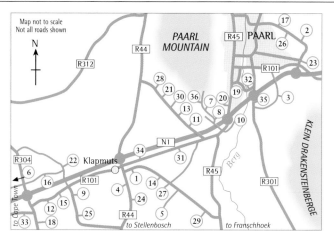

1	ANURA	19	KWV
2	ASHANTI	20	LABORIE
3	AVONDALE	21	LANDSKROON
4	AVONDVREDE	22	LEIDERSBURG
5	BACKSBERG	23	MELLASAT
6	BODEGA	24	MONT DESTIN
7	BRENTHURST	25	MULDERSVLEI
8	COLERAINE	26	NEDERBURG
9	DE MEYE	27	NIEL JOUBERT
10	DE ZOETE INVAL	28	RUITERSVLEI
11	DIAMANT	29	RUPERT & ROTHSCHILD
12	EAGLEVLEI	30	SEIDELBERG
13	FAIRVIEW	31	SIMONSVLEI
14	GLEN CARLOU	32	VENDOME
15	HOOPENBURG	33	VILLIERA
16	JOOSTENBERG	34	WELGEMEEND
17	KLEINVALLEI	35	ZANDDRIFT
18	KOELENHOF	36	ZANDWIJK

Paarl

Scattered premium sites

Half a dozen disconnected sub-regions within the vast municipal area of Paarl provide a wide range of contrasting styles within the classification of Paarl wines. The many small premium winemaking regions located here are separated from each other by the flat alluvial plain of the Berg River and the granite mass of Paarl Mountain and its nature reserve, which broadly slashes through the centre of the district.

In the distant past, Paarl was a prosperous mixed farming area with an important winemaking tradition. When the twin ravages of the initial outbreaks of oidium and phylloxera decimated Cape vineyards, the Paarl district turned to fruit growing, specialising in plums, peaches and table grapes, and largely ignored vineyards for wine production.

The average maximum temperatures in Paarl are somewhat higher than in Stellenbosch and this, together

with the deep, sandy soils along the Berg's flood plain and on Wellington's tributary rivers, effectively combined to ripen table fruits but provided weak, flavourless wines. Though a few small areas continued to grow quality grapes for wine production, these were exceptions to the standard image of Paarl as a production area for simple bulk wines.

As elsewhere in the Western Cape, commercial and competitive success by cellars with favourable terroir in certain areas away from the river plain has stimulated new interest, and Paarl's outer sub-regions have seen widespread replanting of vineyards and the construction of new cellar buildings. In the east the most important vineyards are on the lower foothills of the Simonsberg, where we find Backsberg and Glen Carlou, and across the river on the slopes of the Du Toit's Kloof mountains, where Avondale and Ashanti are making new styles.

1 Avondale farm and the Du Toit's Kloof mountains in late afternoon sunlight.
2 Participants in Paarl's nouveau wine festival.
3&5 These historic town cellars in Paarl are no longer used for winemaking.
4 Grapes waiting to be crushed at the Ashanti cellar alongside a mobile bottling unit.
6 Ashanti's assistant winemaker, Nelson Buthelezi.

In the south-western part of the municipal district, the vineyards of Villiera have changed the understanding of quality influences in Paarl and surrounding areas. Nearby, on the west-facing slopes of Paarl Mountain, there are half a dozen important long, narrow farms, each running from eroded granite soils high on the foothill down to shallow sandy poorly-drained soils as far as a kilometre to the west. Each gradient requires different soil preparation and variety choice. Notable among these elongated farms are Fairview and Landskroon. In West Paarl, between Paarl Mountain and the Paardeberg, clay-rich soils are providing sites for new premium wineries. And finally in North Paarl and parts of Wellington, forty kilometres from Villiera, prizewinning reds are changing long established attitudes.

Red wine is the lifeblood of the Paarl resurgence. As always there are exceptions and chief among these are the delicate and powerful Chardonnay wines from Glen Carlou. But the richness of the clay fraction in the soil and the warm maximum temperatures contribute structure and fruit to skin-fermented wines.

Growing and ripening conditions are fairly similar, despite the great distances and separation between these sub-regions. The southeaster crests the Du Toit's Kloof mountains, lashes through the Ashanti vineyards and disrupts flowering and leaf cover but most of the district receives gentle summer breezes and constant heat during ripening. Soils in the district are various mixtures of sand and decomposed granite. Vines grow without excess vigour on the better winemaking soils, and canopy growth and leaf management is important for the retention of delicacy and freshness.

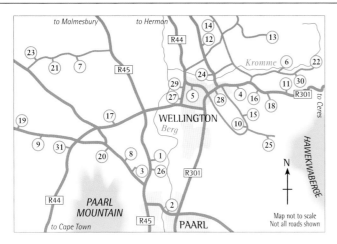

1 BERNHEIM
2 BOLAND (DAL JOSAFAT)
3 BOLAND (N. PAARL)
4 BOVLEI
5 CAPE WINE
6 CLARIDGE
7 DAVID FROST/
  ST CLEMENT
8 DE VILLIERS
9 DOMAINE BRAHMS
10 HILDENBRAND
11 HUGUENOT
12 JACARANDA
13 LINTON PARK
14 MISCHA
15 MONT DU TOIT
16 NAPIER
17 NELSON'S CREEK/NEW BEGINNINGS
18 OUDE WELLINGTON
19 PERDEBERG
20 RHEBOKSKLOOF
21 SCALI
22 SIYABONGA
23 SONOP
24 STORMBERG
25 UPLAND
26 VEENWOUDEN
27 WAMAKERSVALLEI
28 WELGEGUND
29 WELLINGTON
30 WELVANPAS
31 WINDMEUL

Wellington
North Paarl
West Paarl

Long history, new potential

In the pursuit of quality, in the making of better and more complex wines, where do the terms 'hot' and 'cool' – used to describe growing and ripening ambient temperatures – fit? The definitions are so imprecise and the understanding of what works best is so subjective that we're little closer to finding any reasonable rule than we were decades ago with the 'Winkler' system and the use of average maximum temperatures as a guide.

Wellington and North Paarl have high average daily peak temperatures during the growing and ripening seasons. Together with Malmesbury, they have suffered from the trend toward 'cool' areas and have enjoyed a lower level of new investment than most neighbouring districts. This has allowed some Stellenbosch and Franschhoek wineries to obtain red grapes from vineyards on these clay-rich soils from which they have created blockbuster, high-fashion wines. Like Paarl, Wellington suffers from a shortage of well-endowed sites with effectively structured and drained soils and adequate supplies of water in summer. The best sites have

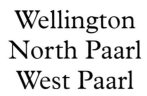

marvellous soils but many vineyards have the limitation of severe water stress during ripening. With the judicious use of irrigation and the effective measuring of soil moisture, farming styles will change and more premium grapes will become available.

If high ripening temperatures have negative effects, what is it that allows so many top red wines to be made from these 'hot country' vineyards? Clearly something else: lower night-time temperatures, lack of plant vigour and naturally small grape sizes can be seen to contribute, but the jury is still out. The continuing market success of Veenwouden's red wines has stifled the original surprise and few now comment on the effect of the temperatures surrounding this estate's ripening grapes.

'What people wanted cooler climates for, historically, doesn't hold true as much as it used to,' says Jason Fisher, the Californian winemaker in charge of West Paarl's St Clement. 'What we look for is productive soils with good deep texture and high clay content. Grapes grown on these soils give really forward-structured red

1 Pieter-Niel Rossouw, winemaker at Mont du Toit.
2 The fermentation cellar at Linton Park.
3 Domaine Brahms.
4 Claridge, on the lower slopes of the Hawequa.
5 Veenwouden's winemaker, Marcel van der Walt.
6 An unusually narrow red fermentation tank at Veenwouden.

wines – rich and powerful, with a brooding weight to them. Wines like this hold up to heavy doses of new wood. I hear that lots of old-school winemakers here want to put their red crush through the mash cooler, to start their red fermentations cold and only hit peak temperatures at the end. I want to do it the other way. There is such wonderful intensity in the red grapes from this area, one needs to start extracting quickly, so I want to get to the maximum temperatures quickly and cool down at the end.'

Gesie Lategan is another newcomer to West Paarl who has revolutionary ideas. Practising as an advocate and married to a judge, Gesie suggests a different way of viewing the evidence provided by soil tests and climatic conditions. Gesie and her husband, Braam, bought Domaine Brahms in 1990 after soil samples showed that this unfashionable area, chiefly planted with wheat, was suitable for wine.

'At that stage everyone seemed to be planting Chardonnay and Sauvignon Blanc. I started preparing the soil for red varieties and my judgement was questioned. Then we were advised to trellis our vines and I hedged my bets by only putting the vineyards that were on best soils onto wires, leaving the weaker soil vineyards as bush vines.

'When the first vineyards of each came into production, it was clear that bush vines (and maybe the weaker soils) were best. We had also been told that the soil on a small area of our farm was too poor to plant vineyards, but we had to do something with this patch. Being a rebel, I planted Shiraz as bush vines and now it's clear that the wine from grapes grown in this block is our very best. And that was completely against the accepted wisdom.

'There's a heartbeat to this land and we should listen to it. This is warm and generous country. We can make outstanding wines in a warm and generous style if we plant what the soil and growing conditions seem to be most comfortable with.'

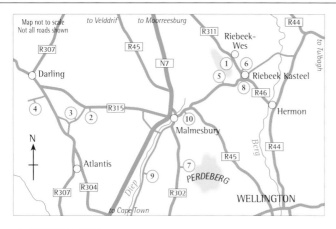

1 ALLESVERLOREN
2 DARLING CELLARS
3 GROENE CLOOF
4 GROOTE POST
5 KLOOVENBURG
6 RIEBEEK
7 LAMMERSHOEK
8 MEERHOF
9 SPICE ROUTE
10 SWARTLAND

1 The cellar at Spice Route.
2 Abé Beukes of Darling Cellars.
3 Vineyards at Riebeek Kasteel.
4 Groote Post, Darling.
5 Charl du Plessis of Spice Route.

Darling
Malmesbury
Paardeberg

Blowing hot and cold

Blazing summer sun, chilled summer nights and the occasional soaking fog: Malmesbury's ripening season contains extreme conditions that can produce blockbuster intensity or haunting elegance.

'When you're facing another day of unrelenting sun, and that blanket of fog rolls in over the Darling Hills from the Atlantic, its like having a water break when you're running a marathon,' says Charl du Plessis, the cellarmaster at Spice Route Winery near Malmesbury, north of Cape Town. 'It doesn't bring water; it just gives us a break. When the vines have had weeks of exposure to direct sun and they can stand for half a day with their crop of high-sugar grapes soaking cold, still fog, you can see and feel the effect.'

There are four different sub-regions within the boundaries of Malmesbury, with wide variations of soil type and climatic conditions for the growing of wine grapes. Unlike other Cape coastal vineyard areas, there are no towering mountain ranges to create variations in sun exposure, and the major differences are created by conditions around the roots and the temperatures surrounding the ripening bunches of grapes.

The two main blocks of deep red shale soil are in the Darling Hills alongside the Atlantic and north of Malmesbury astride the Moreesburg road. Though these soils are equally deep and rich in clay, with efficient moisture-retention and with little variation from a north slope to a south-facing aspect, the coastal vineyards tend

toward supple fruit flavours. The north-eastern neighbours are home to immensely rich tannin and flavour extraction.

Directly east of the Groenekloof – the sea-facing slopes of the Darling Hills – and directly in the path of the morning fog, vineyards are growing in decomposed granite, gravel and sandy soils on the gently rolling hills around Malmesbury.

The northern slopes of the Paardeberg Hills, south-east of Malmesbury, make up the fourth sub-region. This is further inland, has slightly higher rainfall and the vineyards benefit from the underground water table flowing out of the eroded mountain slopes.

The Spice Route Winery harvests grapes in all four districts. 'The area around Malmesbury with granite and gravel soils produces flinty, grassy Sauvignon Blanc, even in dry years, while the big red soils up north tend to give tropical flavours to the wines of this variety. The gravel soils seem to make a good home for Shiraz, while the deep shale is best for Cabernet and Merlot. The extra moisture-holding capacity is needed by the later-ripening varieties. We get the biggest Cabernet Sauvignon and Merlot wines out of this area without really trying, whereas Paardeberg vineyards give us finesse and elegance.'

The Darling-Malmesbury-Paardeberg region has historically been the exclusive preserve of wine co-operatives. While the Swartland Winery remains the largest

producer in the area, crushing 16 000 tons for its many members, there has been a trend in the adjoining Malmesbury and Darling areas towards the growing of speciality premium grapes for an assortment of Stellenbosch and Paarl wine cellars and the simultaneous emergence of local boutique wineries. Warm or cool, this area produces a concentration of fruit rarely found elsewhere in the Cape. Unrelenting summer sun shortens the ripening period.

'The picking date is critical,' says Charl. 'We don't have to wait for sugar – we get more than we need. Vines grow like crazy in these soils and the sugar mounts every day. But we have a short, vivid ripening period between flowering and harvesting, and we have to wait on tenterhooks for ripe skins, ripe pips, ripe tannins before we pick. We have a four-day window between the onset of perfect ripeness and worked fruit.'

Most of the Spice Route's grapes come from the inland belt of vineyards where 40 °C maximum temperatures are not uncommon. The Groote Post Winery, just seven kilometres from the ocean, has different problems to contend with in its Darling Hills vineyards.

'We have only about 20 days a year where the temperature exceeds 30 °C,' says Nick Pentz of Groote Post in the Groenekloof. 'This has some obvious advantages, such as vineyards that are still green and lush about five months after the last real rain, but we have to put up with flowering and budding problems in our Chardonnay, and we have wind that flattens bush vines.'

The farming properties in the Malmesbury and Darling areas are large tracts of land. For hundreds of years they produced wheat and grazed sheep and cattle. Vineyards occupied small blocks near the homestead and many of these near-Atlantic farms carried dairy herds, producing milk for nearby Cape Town.

Recently, the landscape has seen the invasion of huge Caterpillar tractors, deep ripping and mixing powdered lime into the soil in preparation for the patterned order of neat rows of trellised grape vines, kilometres long.

The Darling and Malmesbury districts receive about 450 millimetres of rainfall annually and, as there are no rivers in the vicinity, irrigation is rare. The health of the vineyards in late summer points to the moisture-holding capacity of the clay in the ground.

'In 1997, when I came to Darling Cellars as cellarmaster, I found a lot of surprises,' says Abé Beukes. 'You don't have to do a lot of work in the cellar to soften the tannins in the red grape skins in this area; they come in like that from the vineyard. People who visit here, especially from overseas, think it's a kind of desert and they have the idea that they're going to find harsh, aggressive wines. They ask me where I find the grapes we work with after they taste our wines. I have to explain to them about the quality of the soils in the hills behind this lonely cellar and the surprising effect of the mass of cold ocean water that is out of sight, just over the horizon.'

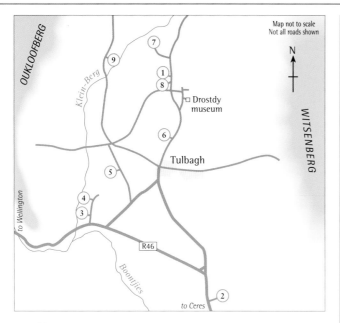

1 DROSTDY
2 DE HEUVEL
3 KLOOFZICHT
4 LEMBERG
5 MONTPELLIER
6 RIJK'S
7 THEUNISKRAAL
8 TULBAGH
9 TWEE JONGE GEZELLEN

1

Tulbagh

Under the stones, a new life

Most of the Tulbagh valley has a thin layer of eroded sandy soil resting on masses of layered rocky material. Until the availability of very large crawler tractors with the strength to break through the stone, only a small part of Tulbagh was able to be cultivated for deep-rooted plants such as vines and fruit trees. This was the narrow band of deep, black alluvial soil along the Klein Berg River, running south close to, and parallel with, the mountain range on the western side of the valley.

Most of Tulbagh has consequently been a grain growing and stock grazing region for its three centuries of farming history. Two events have impacted on the simplicity of this style of life. The first was the development of commercial fruit farming and small-scale vineyards and winemaking on the alluvial river soils during the first half of the twentieth century. The second has started recently as a result of the conversion by powerful, deep-ripping machines of the stony parts of the valley for intensive agricultural use.

Tulbagh soils fit broadly into two zones, granite and sandstone on the west and shale in the east, separated by the fertile river soils. In the northern and western quarter of the valley, between the river and the mountains, owners of successful fruit farms have moved plantations from the black sandy soils into hitherto inaccessible sites

2

among sandstone boulders, breaking previously compacted layers of virtually impenetrable sandstone and other sedimentary rocks.

'We're finding that these subterranean layers of rock contain storehouses of valuable minerals. Now that vine roots can penetrate over a metre down we anticipate richness and complexity in red wines that we've never been able to achieve before,' says Nicky Krone of Twee Jonge Gezellen. This estate became renowned for its fruity white wine in the 1960s and 1970s under the stewardship of N. C. Krone, Nicky's father, from vineyards grown in the sandy river soils. Nicky brought the attention of the world back to the estate with elegant sparkling wines in the 1980s and 1990s. And now red wines made from vines planted in the newly excavated soils will expand interest in Tulbagh's western fringe.

Most of the valley, east of the river, has shallow sandy soils over a massive shale deposit. Deep ripping, which opens up the compacted shale to allow vine root penetration, has shown that Tulbagh could be at the start of a new era, specialising in bold, fruity red wines. Neville Dorrington – a pioneer in the development of the shale part of the valley, historically wheat country – has brought fresh, invigorating attitudes to the formula of farming in Tulbagh. His unwillingness to accept

REVERSING THE CLOCK

Most wine-growing areas around the world have spells of intensely hot weather during mid- and late summer, and the Cape is no exception. Particularly in mountain-enclosed basins such as the Tulbagh, Paarl, Franschhoek and Worcester valleys, temperatures can become scorching, and when grapes harvested on an excessively hot day are crushed, the resulting juice would normally enter the fermentation cycle at a high temperature. As warm grape juice quickly loses its precious aroma and flavour content, most production cellars use chilling facilities to reduce the temperature of juice extracted from grapes brought in from the vineyards on especially hot days.

The juice from grapes picked under cooler conditions requires less emergency care, and several Cape wine estates have pioneered harvesting grapes during the night hours, when temperatures are at their lowest in the 24-hour daily cycle. At Twee Jonge Gezellen and at the nearby Rijk's vineyard in the Tulbagh valley and at L'Ormarins near Franschhoek, grapes are picked by the light of battery-powered lamps and the moon.

For two months every year the staff of Twee Jonge Gezellen, numbering more than a hundred people, wake in the late afternoon and head off into the vineyards or into the cellar to work as the twilight fades. Throughout the night they go through the stages of the vineyard-to-cellar cycle, cutting the ripe bunches from the vines, transporting the grapes to the cellar, operating the crushing machinery and setting the fermentation process in motion. When the sun rises over the Witzenberg Mountains above Tulbagh, it shines on the Twee Jonge Gezellen team heading home for a good day's sleep.

3

1 Night harvesting at Twee Jonge Gezellen.
2 Nicky Krone, Twee Jonge Gezellen's owner and cellarmaster.
3&5 The cellar and vineyards at Rijk's.
4 The Cape winelands are home to many characterful individuals.

restrictions has created striking vineyards and equally impressive red wines with structure and fruit characteristics previously unknown in Tulbagh. Dorrington's Rijk's Cellar has made a list of prizewinning wines from maiden vintages. These sell at prices previously unknown in Tulbagh, a town that was visited chiefly for its guesthouses and stately Cape Dutch buildings.

'People have completely misunderstood Tulbagh,' says Pierre Wahl, cellarmaster at Rijk's. 'They have tried to guess why red wines made in the past haven't been better and have concluded that Tulbagh must be too hot. We measure everything, and we've found that nights are so cold here that our average daily summer temperatures are lower than those of many more famous places.'

All grapes at both Twee Jonge Gezellen and Rijk's are picked at night. 'The average temperature of the juice we draw off newly crushed grapes is 13°C, and that's in January and February,' says Pierre. As a result of these developments, new boutique cellars are sprouting up all over the Tulbagh valley. Before long, the Tulbagh wine route will have over 20 members and at least half of them will be in the shale soils section where until recently the only summer activity was the waving of wheat in the gentle south-east winds.

4

5

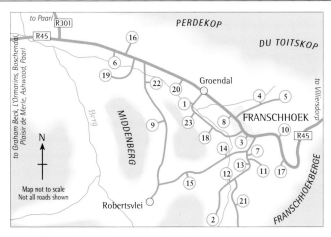

1 Franschhoek is renowned for its restaurants.
2 Angels surround the door of the cellar at Agusta.
3 Achim von Arnim of Cabrière.
4 Emblem of the Vignerons de Franschhoek.
5 The L'Ormarins homestead.
6 Haute Cabrière's wood maturation cellar.

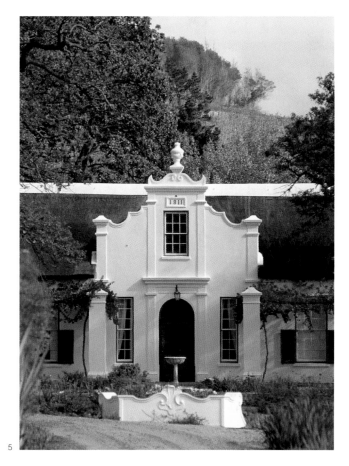

Franschhoek

In and out of the shade

Lying in a relatively remote area of the Cape, bordered on three sides by mountains, the Franschhoek Valley was at one time known as Olifantshoek ('Elephant's Corner'). Elephants found its isolation ideal for raising their young and were often seen there by early European settlers. The first farms granted in Franschhoek were settled in the final decade of the seventeenth century and were granted to Swiss, German, Dutch and French settlers.

Most of the early farms were about 60 hectares in extent and were situated along the Franschhoek River, a tributary of the Berg River. Mixed farming including the growing of grape vines for the production of wine was carried out on these mostly sandy alluvial soils.

Today, Franschhoek's vineyards have spread further up the mountain slopes and grapes are grown under varying conditions, affected chiefly by altitude, aspect toward the sun and the quantity of clay in the soil. Higher vineyards tend to have higher rainfall, less direct sun and more clay in the soil.

'We can be working up in our top vineyards in heavy

jackets and go down to the village and have people laugh at us because of the way we're dressed. It can be cold, wet and windy up there, and mild and dry down below,' says Peter Arnold, cellarmaster at Chamonix, one of the few farms high on the south-facing slopes. 'You can't believe there's such a difference in climate in areas that are so close together. Our top vineyards have a long interval between flowering and harvest, and I believe that even Pinot Noir will be able to reach adequate maturity there.'

The vineyards on this southern slope have less direct sun each day than elsewhere in the valley. In some cases, the bright rays of the sun first highlight the luminous green of vineyard leaves on these hillsides around mid-morning, while the other side of the valley has been bathed in energy-producing sunlight for several hours.

These upper slope vineyards on the south-facing mountains also face the strongest effect of the south-east wind. Uniquely among Western Cape winter-rainfall vineyard sites, this area is occasionally exposed to the

light summer rains of Walker Bay, when the southeaster rolls over the Villiersdorp-Franschhoek pass. These summer winds can reduce the efficiency of the vines' flowering, thus reducing the crop.

Wind, unseasonable rain and cold temperatures have a less obvious effect on vineyards on the north-facing slopes and on the valley floor. In these locations, moisture retention in the soil during long periods of summer sun, without rain, is probably the most important influence on grape and wine quality. The borders of the hillside pine forests are continually receding uphill as new land at ever-higher altitudes is prepared for planting vines.

Roughly speaking, the valley is cigar-shaped, running east to west, with a warmer and more generous climate in the lower reaches. Dieu Donné, one of the few farms on the south-facing slopes at the head of the valley, incorporated a new vineyard in the lower, north-facing section, ten kilometres to the south-west and has found that red varieties from here produce a different

style of wine, reaching riper tannin levels more easily with less pronounced acidity. The valley's best soils appear to be produced from decomposed granite. Clay rich, these enable vineyards to thrive through long rainless summer periods.

Franschhoek has become a major tourist attraction in the Western Cape, and the traditional wineries, mostly sited on the valley floor on the original farms, conduct a healthy trade with visitors. Boschendal, just beyond the valley proper, receives over 150 000 tourists each year and employs more than 100 people to serve them.

Chamonix, which also houses a highly rated restaurant, sells over one-third of its wines to people visiting the farm. The original peace and quiet that attracted the elephant matriarchs to the valley has largely disappeared along with the giant mammals and has been replaced by the hum of cars and commerce.

1 The Franschhoek valley seen from the north-east.
2&3 Franschhoek has a thriving hospitality industry.
4 Eighty-five farmers belong to the local co-operative winery.
5 Chamonix's barrel cellar.
6 A family tree in the Franschhoek museum.

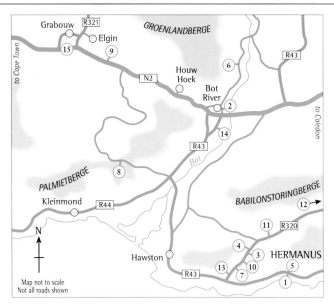

1 Harvesting at Hamilton Russell.
2 Paul Cluver Estate, Elgin.
3 The Hemel-en-Aarde Valley from Sumaridge.
4 Peter Finlayson of Bouchard Finlayson.
5 WhaleHaven cellar.
6 Bouchard Finlayson, Hemel-en-Aarde Valley.

Walker Bay

Close to the ocean

There are three distinct grape-growing areas in the Walker Bay ward of the Overberg. In time, each of these will probably earn its own classification and there may well be more than three sub-regions.

'We get more direct sun here in Bot River than growers in the nearby Hemel-en-Aarde Valley and Elgin regions,' says Niels Verburg, cellarmaster at Beaumont Wines. 'We get the same cooling wind off the sea, but the other two growing areas spend many days completely covered in cloud during summer, and this usually misses us.'

Walker Bay is named after the gulf of water offshore beside the town of Hermanus, near the junction of the Indian and Atlantic Oceans. The winemaking region carrying this name is sandwiched between Stellenbosch to the west and Robertson/Klein Karoo to the north, and contains varied topography and climatic conditions.

The Elgin-Grabouw region is spread across the narrow plateau above the Hottentots Holland Mountains, south-east of the town of Stellenbosch. Descending a winding pass from Elgin to the level, rolling wheat and barley fields indicates that a different set of growing conditions apply in Bot River. To the south-east, near the seaside town of Hermanus, the maritime influences over wind and cloud-cover in the Hemel-en-Aarde Valley create yet another forum for flavour development in winemaking.

'That ocean,' says Kevin Grant of Hamilton Russell, 'is our air-conditioner. We may not get the blasting southeaster of Somerset West, but we get a daily breeze off the sea, which is just two kilometres away, all through summer.'

The Walker Bay region is a few points of latitude further south than Stellenbosch and average summer temperatures are a degree or two lower.

'We have gentle temperatures,' says Peter Finlayson, cellarmaster of Bouchard Finlayson Wines, also in the Hemel-en-Aarde Valley. 'You can't say it's cool, like Champagne or New Zealand's south island, as we get some really hot days in summer. Everything is moderate; nothing is extreme here.'

Elgin, however, has high rainfall and the Western Cape's shortest period of daily average direct sun.

'You have to choose vineyard sites carefully and with some experience,' says Neil Ellis of Neil Ellis Wines, a long-time Elgin grape purchaser. 'You need to find sites that have soil with high clay content and maximum sun exposure. And I believe that early-maturing varieties like Pinot Noir are going to be the core of this area's future success.'

Whether just above sea level, as in the Hemel-en-Aarde Valley, or at the altitudes of Elgin, each grower and winemaker has to manage what the soil and environment provides.

'It's just like cricket. You have to play this game ball by ball,' says Peter Finlayson. 'Every block of vineyard, every year, comes into the cellar a little different. You have to wait for it and you have to play it as it comes. Naturally, you have a whole year to help the vineyard do its best. Then you accept what comes and you handle it on its merit. You can't do anything about yesterday or tomorrow.'

Whereas Elgin and Hemel-en-Aarde show affinity

3

toward the so-called 'Eskimo' varieties of Chardonnay, Sauvignon Blanc and Pinot Noir, Bot River, with its additional sun hours, has clear potential for full-bodied, powerfully structured reds.

'I think that Shiraz is shaping up as our most promising variety,' says Niels Verburg. 'All of the classic, thicker-skinned reds get deep colour and rich, soft tannins here, and the majority of new vineyards being planted in Bot River are from Bordeaux and Rhône-origin red varieties.'

Walker Bay is one of the newer planets in the Cape's wine universe, and the area has advanced from a curiosity to a serious contributor to quality wines.

5

4

6

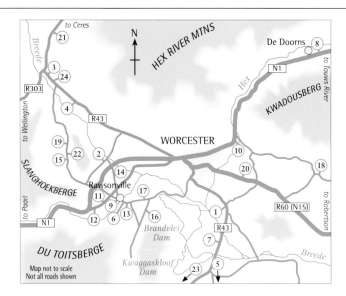

1 The Worcester valley from the Slanghoek
   co-operative winery.
2 Open fermenters and tank press at Deetlefs Estate.
3 Some Rawsonville soils have a high stone density.
4 The vineyards of Opstal Estate.
5 The Cape Dutch homestead on Deetlefs Estate.
6 Nuy winery, celebrated for its muscadels.

Worcester

Moving up the slopes

2
3
4
5

In volume of juice and wine, Worcester is South Africa's biggest grape producing area. Vines are grown for wine-making on the broad valley floor on both sides of the Breede River, and increasingly in the foothills of the surrounding mountains as market dynamics push growers away from mass production of simple wines.

The Worcester valley is long and wide. The western end provides a comparatively narrow entry channel for the Breede River and as one travels eastward with its flow the valley floor widens to over 30 kilometres of alluvial river flats, covered by a network of vineyards, orchards and small, mixed farms.

This same east-west journey, taking you from the lashing winter rains of Slanghoek and Wolseley to the semi-arid countryside of Agterkliphoogte and Overhex, can be accomplished in a 30 minute car trip, all within one valley.

The river flood plain has deep, black, sandy soils and can support a very large crop on each vine. These vineyards were planned and planted to produce brandy and contain almost exclusively white wine varieties.

'Worcester has seen major changes in the last five years,' says Stanley Louw of the Opstal Estate, in Slanghoek. 'New red plantings now outnumber the new plantings of white vines, particularly where soils indicate the potential for high quality juice.'

By moving one's attention around the outer limits of the valley one can locate pockets of special soil and climate that differ widely from each other, indicating a future need for clear differentiation. 'The western end of the valley, where rainfall is so heavy, has tremendous diversity in soils that can vary many times even in one vineyard block,' says Stanley Louw. 'This means we have to work hard, conducting trials and experiments to find the best variety for each location.'

The west and south-west corner of the valley, from Wolseley to Rawsonville, is flanked by high mountain ranges that not only bring rain but also reduce daily average hours of direct sunlight. Though peak summer temperatures are fairly high in this sector, nights are cold and average daily temperatures are lower than those of many more fashionable Cape wine producing regions. The sloping soils of the Slanghoek foothills vary in texture from loamy with a stone fraction to a concentrated mix of gravel and stone that looks more like a road than agricultural land. Ascending the foothills, the new plantings are in soils that are richly coloured with clay and have valuable moisture retention capacity, allowing the vine's roots to find water naturally during ripening.

Irrigated water is the lifeblood of Worcester as it is in most Cape inland areas. While it assists Slanghoek and Rawsonville farmers to reduce vineyard stress in late summer, irrigation is vital for the life of vines in the lower rainfall areas in the northern and eastern parts of the valley and, of course, all over the flood plain.

Soils in the west and south contain mostly sand and granite particles, with clay on mountain slopes. In the northern and eastern ends of the valley, where winter rain clouds are seldom seen, limestone appears in the soil and creates high acidity in juice and wines.

Strong winds are not part of Worcester's climatic pattern. Isolated pockets are mildly affected by the southeaster and this wind brings some rain in summer to the semi-arid red Karoo and sandy lime soils at the eastern end of the valley.

It seems that Worcester as a whole will continue to produce chiefly white wines as the majority of the flood plain soils are not suited to red varieties. The new red vineyards are being planted in the fringes of the valley, chiefly in Wolseley and Slanghoek and on the far eastern hill slopes.

6

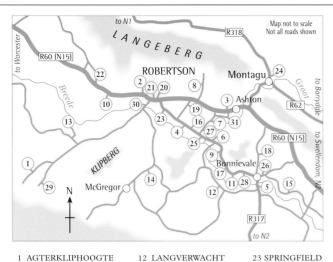

Map not to scale
Not all roads shown

1 AGTERKLIPHOOGTE	12 LANGVERWACHT	23 SPRINGFIELD
2 APPELSDRIFT	13 LE GRAND CHASSEUR	24 UITVLUCHT
2 ASHTON	14 MCGREGOR	25 VAN LOVEREN
4 BON COURAGE	15 MERWESPONT	26 VAN ZYLSHOF
5 BONNIEVALE	16 MON DON	27 VILJOENSDRIFT
6 DE WETSHOF	17 MOOIUITSIG	28 WELTEVREDE
7 EXCELSIOR	18 NORDALE	29 WINDFALL
8 FRAAI UITZICHT	19 RIETVALLEI	30 WONDERFONTEIN
9 GOEDVERWACHT	20 ROBERTSON	31 ZANDVLIET
10 GRAHAM BECK MADEBA	21 ROODEZANDT	
11 JONKHEER	22 ROOIBERG	

Robertson

Red revolution in white country

The white wine citadel of Robertson is under attack from within as red vineyards are being planted on every slope. In an area where farmers measured only the sweetness and volume of the crop before the harvest, they now have to assess the development of colour and tannin in the skins.

Planned and developed as vineyard country for shiploads of white wine by administrators shaping the South African wine industry in the mid-twentieth century, Robertson became a major resource centre for dry white wine for brandy production and sweet fortified Muscadel wines for the South African palates of the time. The water in the Brandvlei Dam at Worcester first encouraged fruit orchards on the wide, fertile plains along the Breede River, and broad reaches of Colombard, Chenin Blanc and Muscadel followed. South Africa's favourite tipple, brandy, required large volumes of economically grown white wine to provide raw material for distillation. The fertile soils of Robertson, infused with limestone, were well suited to supply the light, acid wines needed. After planting vines of the recommended specialist brandy varieties, Colombard and Ugri Blanc, winemakers found themselves with surprising results in the tanks. Robertson Colombard made remarkably aromatic and zesty wines when harvested for low alcohol distillation. This created a new market and Robertson added dry white wines to the objectives set for each harvest. In time, this led to the planting of Chenin Blanc

and, eventually, Chardonnay and Sauvignon Blanc. The team at De Wetshof pioneered the latter varieties.

Danie de Wet's leadership and commercial success encouraged other Robertson growers to follow suit. During the 1990s the grape-growing, wine-marketing community of the district formed the Robertson Wine Trust to develop and promote the area and its wines. Though commercial success with Chardonnay can be found in most Cape wine regions, this variety has made itself at home in Robertson, where it successfully produces many styles of wine. The Wine Trust, with its technical workshops for growers and winemakers and a co-ordinated programme of regional marketing, has developed tourism and Robertson's exposure to international wine buyers.

A sense of community is more evident in Robertson than it is in most other Cape winemaking regions. Competing farmers work together for their common benefit. That the lime in Robertson's soil and the afternoon south-easterly wind brings special qualities to the ripening grapes has long been accepted, but the Trust is taking this further.

'We have more respect for these things now,' says Danie de Wet. 'We want to know what the limestone does for the plant and under what conditions.'

The southerly wind's influence on Robertson is another focus of study as almost all of the Cape's vineyards are ventilated by this prevailing summer wind.

1 Junior league football in Robertson.
2 The cellar at Springfield Estate, Robertson.
3 Irrigation is the lifeblood of all farming activity
   in the dry Breede River valley.
4 Van Loveren, one of more than 30 wineries
   in the Robertson-Ashton-Bonnievale area.

'The highest peaks of the Riviersonderend Mountains lie between the Indian Ocean and Robertson,' says Abri Bruwer of Robertson. 'To get here, the wind has to ascend this range to reach the best part of 2 000 metres in altitude. It loses 3 °C for every 300 metres it rises above sea level to crest the mountains at about 10 °C. When it arrives down here in the middle of the valley, 200 metres above sea level, at noon on a midsummer's day it has reached about 20 °C. You can feel the temperature drop on most days around midday. Now we're studying how and when this affects our crop and the quality of its juice.'

The Robertson Wine Trust has linked the 24 weather stations located on individual farms with the nation's weather service, to better predict the likelihood of ideal conditions for the outbreak of fungal diseases. Armed with this information daily, Robertson grape growers have been able to decrease the number and volumes of preventative sprays, without risk to the vines or crop.

Blocked by mountain ranges to the north and west, Robertson misses out on most of the regular winter rainfall enjoyed by the coastal grape-growing areas. With only 200 millimetres of rain a year, this semi-arid climate forces farmers to irrigate all their vineyards regularly. Whereas this used to be seen as an automatic supplement to volumes, sophisticated skills in computer-controlled and monitored water supply have enabled growers to have greater control over moisture supply to

vineyards than their colleagues in dry-land vineyard regions. They have more influence over the health of the vine and its crop.

Higher prices paid for red grapes than their white counterparts caused Robertson's vineyard owners to plant red varieties in their previously exclusive white wine terrain. This soon became a major issue for the Wine Trust. A workshop revealed a widespread lack of knowledge of red grape physiology. No one could understand why healthy red grapes grown under irrigation in Robertson's fertile soils should not produce tannin-rich red wines similar to their coastal counterparts. International consultants were employed to study the problem and find solutions. Robertson's red vineyard project has been in process for several years now and striking results can be found under several brands.

'Our red vineyards are moving out of the valley floor, up the hills,' says Paul de Wet of Zandvliet. 'Where things grow like wildfire in our sandy river soils, they struggle in the limestone clay of the kalkveld and there is much more impact and concentration. And we only give water when we know the plant needs it.'

Time will measure the success of red wine in Robertson, but the community will make sure that it has a real chance.

4

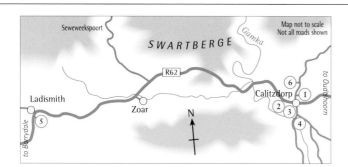

Map not to scale
Not all roads shown

Calitzdorp

Any port in a storm

One of the most interesting centres of quality wine production in the Cape is located in the tiny inland town of Calitzdorp. While the rest of fine wine production is located within an hour-and-a-half's drive from Cape Town, the home of South African port-style wines (now known as Cape Ruby) is half a day away to the east, in a completely different climatic zone, with a contrasting way of life.

Calitzdorp is a quaint country dorp, with general stores and furniture shops, astride the Gamka River, which is prone to potentially catastrophic summer floods. The only visual changes in twenty years of town life have resulted from the gradual acceptance of the popularity of its port-style wines. The traditional country pubs once devoted to the brandy drinking culture of rural South Africa, now reflect appeals to the Cape Ruby connoisseur, with changes to name and décor. Gracious town homes have been converted to guesthouses replete with signage reflecting the town's best-known product. These colourful changes to this otherwise unremarkable town paralleled the introduction of the Calitzdorp Wine Route in 1979 and the annual South African Port Festival.

Bound to the banks of the river by the umbilical cords of irrigation channels and pipelines, agricultural activity concentrated on fruit, including table grapes and wine grapes for the production of mainly sweet wines.

Originally pastoral land, sprinkled with sheep and

ostriches, the Calitzdorp area gained added prosperity when cultivation of the alluvial flatlands along the river became possible. And nothing is likely to have disturbed the way of life in this village if two local boys from the Nel family, cousins with identical initials, hadn't brought entrepreneurial ideas back from university.

Carel and Boets Nel's fathers were brothers, farming like all their neighbours with stone fruit and grapes. Both made sweet wine chiefly from Muscadel and Muscat d'Alexandrie for the South African domestic market. Carel and Boets saw that the world trend towards fine quality wines could bring added prosperity to the district and started to change the ways their fathers had always done business. Vineyards were planted with new varieties like Sauvignon Blanc, Chardonnay and Cabernet Sauvignon, and the cellars were modified to allow cold fermentation and barrel maturation.

But Calitzdorp has a severe climate with extremes that test the ability of any cellarmaster to retain delicate grape flavours in a dry wine. First Carel and then his cousin began to pay attention to making better versions of what was known as South African port wine, with partially fermented juice of red grapes and light fortification with wine spirit.

Calitzdorp is just one of many South African winemaking regions where cellarmasters try to emulate the esteemed semi-fermented sweet wines of Portugal. The focused attentions of the Nel cousins and the specialised

1 Ostriches and vineyards share space in the rugged landscape around Calitzdorp.
2 Vineyards in the flood plain of the Gamka River.
3 The Calitzdorp Dam provides essential water for local farmers.
4 Boets Nel, Tony Mossop and Carel Nel.

growing conditions of the area have combined to establish this district as South Africa's Cape Ruby capital.

Whereas the Cape coastal grape-growing regions have a Mediterranean-style climate, with most rain falling in the vine's dormant winter phase, Calitzdorp is located on the boundary between winter and summer rainfall regions. Long months of blue skies and extended periods of drought are the norm in this semi-arid landscape and the rainy spells in March-April and September-October are insufficient for permanent agriculture without irrigation. Infrequent rain clouds are less important to Calitzdorp Cape Ruby-makers than the long periods of hot sun.

A year in Calitzdorp is notable for high maximum summer temperatures, with many days exceeding 35 °C, and very cold winter nights, often bringing frost. Hot summers and cold winter nights are common in the Cape interior, leading one to look at the soil and geological influences behind the rise of Calitzdorp's unique Cape Ruby reputation. In search of greater intensity and concentration of fruit flavours and tannins in the selected varieties, Carel and Boets moved their vineyards from the fertile alluvial plain, where the sweet wine grapes had always been grown, to higher ground where the vines struggle to ripen a big crop in the lime-rich, stony soil and yields have to be carefully restrained to achieve the desired sugar levels.

Boets and Carel have found that the best flavours are found in vineyards grown in soils containing vertical strata of shale, which seems to be unique to the area. After experimenting with many soil types they have planted most of the varieties preferred by the originators of this style of wine in Portugal. These varieties, including Touriga Naçional, Souzão and Tinta Roriz, have fine tannin character in the grape skins and are able to ripen their fruit to high levels of sugar without creating raisins.

Winemaking follows Portugal's traditional open-fermentation techniques, with additional steps of mash chilling and cold maceration of the pulp for better colour extraction, until the introduction of almost pure distilled grape spirit approximately halfway through fermentation. This has an instant effect on the yeast activity, halting the conversion of the sugar and producing a sweet wine with about 20% alcohol. After allowing the yeast and other solids to settle, the liquid is drained off into old, many-times-used wine barrels of various sizes for up to two years of maturation. Like their port-making counterparts in the northern hemisphere, the Nel cousins produce many styles of Cape Ruby, from rich, soft ruby to tannin-rich vintage styles on their respective farms – Carel at Boplaas and Boets at Die Krans.

In time, these wines will have to develop their own identities and survive without the port appellation, which will be forbidden to South African producers from the 2005 vintage. Though special permission will allow the retention of the foreign name in South African domestic distribution until 2012, Boplaas and Die Krans labels will rely on reputation to identify their styles of wine.   *

3

4

Bellingham.

Roggeland Country House.

One of several dining venues at Spier.

Zevenwacht's homestead is now a restaurant.

Visitors' guide

The entries below contain essential information for visitors about a selection of wineries that are within easy driving distance of Cape Town. Full details of all the producers in the country can be found in two annual publications: *John Platter's South African Wines* and *Wine Magazine's Pocket Guide to the Wines and Cellars of South Africa*. These books also provide a review of restaurants in the winelands. Please note that many wineries are closed on Sundays and public holidays, and that not all have appropriate facilities for disabled visitors.

CONSTANTIA ▦

DURBANVILLE ▦

STELLENBOSCH ▦

FRANSCHHOEK/SIMONDIUM ▦

PAARL ▦

HELDERBERG ▦

Buitenverwachting MAP P. 122

TEL: 021 794 5190
TASTINGS/SALES:
  MON–FRI 09:00–17:00
  SAT 09:00–13:00
TOURS: BY APPOINTMENT
RESTAURANT: TEL 021 794 3522
  LUNCH & DINNER TUE–FRI; DINNER SAT
PICNICS: BASKETS AVAILABLE IN SEASON
ACCOMMODATION: NO

Constantia Uitsig MAP P. 122

TEL: 021 794 1810
TASTINGS/SALES:
  MON–FRI 09:00–17:30
  SAT 09:30–16:00
  SUN 10:00–16:00
TOURS: BY APPOINTMENT
RESTAURANTS:
  CONSTANTIA UITSIG TEL 021 794 4480
  LA COLOMBE TEL 021 794 2390
  SPAANSCHEMAT RIVER CAFÉ
  TEL 021 794 3010
PICNICS: NO
ACCOMMODATION:
  COUNTRY LODGE TEL 021 794 6500

Groot Constantia MAP P. 122

TEL: 021 794 5128
TASTINGS/SALES:
  IN SEASON, MON–SUN 09:00–18:00
  OUT OF SEASON, MON–SUN 10:00–17:00
TOURS:
  IN SEASON, EVERY HOUR 10:00–16:00
  OUT OF SEASON, 11:00, 15:00 & 16:00
RESTAURANTS:
  JONKERSHUIS TEL 021 794 6255
    MON 10:00–16:30; TUE–SAT 09:00–22:00; SUN
    09:00–17:00
  TAVERN TEL 021 794 1144
    SUN–MON 09:00–17:00; CLOSED MON OUT OF
    SEASON
    TUE–SAT 09:00–11:00
PICNICS: AVAILABLE FOR PURCHASE OR
  BRING YOUR OWN
ACCOMMODATION: NO

Klein Constantia MAP P. 122

TEL: 021 794 5188
TASTINGS/SALES:
  MON–FRI 09:00–17:00
  SAT 09:00–13:00
TOURS: BY APPOINTMENT
RESTAURANT: NO
PICNICS: NO
ACCOMMODATION: NO

Steenberg MAP P. 122

TEL: 021 713 2211
TASTINGS/SALES:
  IN SEASON, MON–FRI 09:00–16:30;
  SAT 09:00–13:00
TOURS: MON–FRI BY APPOINTMENT
RESTAURANT: TEL 021 713 2222
PICNICS: NO
ACCOMMODATION:
  COUNTRY HOTEL: TEL 021 713 2222

Altydgedacht MAP P. 124

TEL: 021 976 1295
TASTINGS/SALES:
  MON–FRI 09:00–17:00
  SAT 09:00–13:00
TOURS: BY APPOINTMENT
RESTAURANT:
  PAMPOENKRAAL (FUNCTIONS ONLY)
  TEL 021 913 4962
PICNICS: NO
ACCOMMODATION: NO

Bloemendal MAP P. 124

TEL: 021 976 2682
TASTINGS/SALES:
  MON–FRI 09:00–17:00
  SAT 09:00–13:00
TOURS: NO
RESTAURANT: TEL 021 975 7575
PICNICS: NO
ACCOMMODATION: NO

Diemersdal MAP P. 124

TEL: 021 976 3361
TASTINGS/SALES:
  MON–FRI 09:00–17:00
  SAT 09:00–15:00
TOURS: IN SEASON BY APPOINTMENT
RESTAURANT: NO
PICNICS: BASKETS AVAILABLE BY
  ARRANGEMENT
ACCOMMODATION: NO

Durbanville Hills MAP P. 124

TEL: 021 558 1300
TASTINGS/SALES:
  MON–FRI 09:00–16:30
  SAT 10:00–14:30
  SUN 10:00–14:00
TOURS:
  MON–FRI 11:00 & 15:00
RESTAURANT: FUNCTION VENUE (@ THE HILLS)
PICNICS: BASKETS AVAILABLE NOV–FEB
ACCOMMODATION: NO

Meerendal MAP P. 124

TEL: 021 975 1655
TASTINGS/SALES:
  MON–FRI 09:00–17:00
  SAT 09:00–13:00
TOURS: NO
RESTAURANT: FUNCTION VENUE
PICNICS: NO
ACCOMMODATION: NO

Nitida MAP P. 124

TEL: 021 976 1467
TASTINGS/SALES:
  MON–FRI 09:00–17:00
  SAT 09:30–12:30
TOURS: NO
RESTAURANT: NO
PICNICS: NO
ACCOMMODATION: NO

Amani MAP P. 130

TEL: 021 905 1126
TASTINGS/SALES:
  TUE–SAT 10:00–16:00
TOURS: BY APPOINTMENT
RESTAURANT: NO
PICNICS: BRING YOUR OWN
ACCOMMODATION: NO

Asara MAP P. 130

TEL: 021 886 5884
TASTINGS/SALES:
  MON–FRI 09:00–17:00
  SAT, NOV–APR 10:00–17:00
  SAT, MAY–OCT 10:00–14:00
TOURS: BY APPOINTMENT
RESTAURANT: NO
PICNICS: BRING YOUR OWN
ACCOMMODATION: NO

Blaauwklippen MAP P. 126

TEL: 021 880 0133
TASTINGS/SALES:
  MON–FRI 09:00–17:00
  SAT 09:00–13:00
TOURS: BY APPOINTMENT
RESTAURANT:
  CAPE KITCHEN @ BLAAUWKLIPPEN
  TEL 021 880 0977
  LUNCH MON–SAT
PICNICS: NO
ACCOMMODATION: NO

A range of fine cuisine is offered in the winelands.

The main restaurant at Boschendal.

Grande Roche, Paarl.

The buffet lunch at Boschendal.

Delaire
MAP P. 128

TEL: 021 885 1756
TASTINGS/SALES:
    MON–FRI 09:00–17:00
    SAT 10:00–17:00
    SUN 10:00–16:00
TOURS: BY APPOINTMENT
RESTAURANT:
    THE GREEN DOOR TEL 021 885 1149
    LUNCH JUN–AUG
    LUNCH & DINNER SEP–APR
PICNICS: BASKETS AVAILABLE SEP–APR
ACCOMMODATION:
    MOUNTAIN LODGES, SELF-CATERING

Delheim
MAP P. 128

TEL: 021 882 2033
TASTINGS/SALES:
    MON–FRI 09:00–17:00
    SAT, OCT–APR 09:00–15:00
    SUN, OCT–APR 11:30–15:00
TOURS:
    MON–FRI 10:30 & 14:30
    SAT 10:30
RESTAURANT:
    DELHEIM GARDEN RESTAURANT
    TEL 021 882 2297
    MON–FRI 12:00–14:30
    SAT & SUN, OCT–APR 12:00–14:30
PICNICS: NO
ACCOMMODATION: NO

Hartenberg
MAP P. 132

TEL: 021 865 2541
TASTINGS/SALES:
    MON–FRI 09:00–17:00
    SAT 10:00–17:00
TOURS: NO
RESTAURANT: TEL AS ABOVE
    MON–SAT 12:00–14:00
PICNICS: NO
ACCOMMODATION: NO

Hazendal
MAP P. 132

TEL: 021 903 5112
TASTINGS/SALES:
    MON–FRI 08:30–16:30
    SAT 09:30–15:00
    SUN 10:00–15:00
TOURS:
    MON–FRI 11:00 & 15:00
RESTAURANT:
    HERMITAGE TEL: 021 903 5112
    MON–SUN 12:00–14:30
PICNICS: BASKETS AVAILABLE
ACCOMMODATION: NO

Kanonkop
MAP P. 128

TEL: 021 884 4656
TASTINGS/SALES:
    MON–FRI 08:30–17:00
    SAT 08:30–12:30
TOURS: BY APPOINTMENT
RESTAURANT: NO
PICNICS: NO
ACCOMMODATION: NO

Kleine Zalze
MAP P. 126

TEL: 021 880 0717
TASTINGS/SALES:
    MON–FRI 09:00–17:00
    SAT 11:00–16:00
TOURS: BY APPOINTMENT
RESTAURANT: TEL 021 880 0862
    LUNCH MON–SAT
PICNICS: BASKETS AVAILABLE
ACCOMMODATION:
    GUEST COTTAGES

Laibach
MAP P. 128

TEL: 021 884 4511
TASTINGS/SALES:
    MON–FRI 09:00–17:00
    SAT 09:00–13:00
TOURS: BY APPOINTMENT
RESTAURANT: NO
PICNICS: NO
ACCOMMODATION: NO

Lanzerac
MAP P. 126

TEL: 021 886 5641
TASTINGS/SALES:
    MON–FRI 10:00–16:30
    SAT 10:00–14:00
TOURS:
    MON–FRI 11:00 & 15:00
RESTAURANTS:
    GOVERNOR'S HALL & TERRACE TEL 021 887 1132
    B'FAST, LUNCH & DINNER MON–SUN
PICNICS: BRING YOUR OWN
ACCOMMODATION:
    HOTEL TEL 021 887 1132

L'Avenir
MAP P. 128

TEL: 021 889 5001
TASTINGS/SALES:
    MON–FRI 10:00–17:00
    SAT 10:00–16:00
TOURS: BY APPOINTMENT
RESTAURANT: NO
PICNICS: NO
ACCOMMODATION:
    GUEST HOUSE FAX 021 889 7313

Lievland
MAP P. 128

TEL: 021 875 5226
TASTINGS/SALES:
    MON–FRI 09:00–17:00
    SAT 09:00–13:00
TOURS: BY APPOINTMENT
RESTAURANT: NO
PICNICS: BRING YOUR OWN
ACCOMMODATION: NO

Meerlust
MAP P. 134

TEL: 021 843 3587
TASTINGS/SALES:
    MON–THU 09:00–17:00
    FRI 09:00–16:30
TOURS: BY APPOINTMENT
RESTAURANT: NO
PICNICS: NO
ACCOMMODATION: NO

Morgenhof
MAP P. 128

TEL: 021 889 5510
TASTINGS/SALES:
    OUT OF SEASON, MON–FRI 09:00–16:30; SAT & SUN 10:00–15:00
    IN SEASON, MON–FRI 09:00–17:30; SAT & SUN 10:00–17:00
TOURS: MATURATION CELLAR VIEWING
RESTAURANT: TEL AS ABOVE
    WINTER DAILY 12:00–14:30
    SUMMER DAILY 12:00–15:00
COFFEE SHOP: TEL AS ABOVE
    WINTER, MON–SUN 09:00–16:30
    SUMMER, MON–SUN 09:00–17:30
PICNICS: NO
ACCOMMODATION: NO

Neethlingshof
MAP P. 130

TEL: 021 883 8988
TASTINGS/SALES:
    MAR–NOV, MON–FRI 09:00–17:00
    MAR–APR, SAT & SUN 10:00–16:00
    DEC–FEB, MON–FRI 09:00–19:00
    DEC–FEB, SAT & SUN 10:00–18:00
TOURS: BY APPOINTMENT
RESTAURANTS:
    THE LORD NEETHLING &
    THE PALM TERRACE TEL 021 883 8966
    TUE–SAT 09:00–22:00; SUN & MON 09:00–16:00
PICNICS: BRING YOUR OWN
ACCOMMODATION: NO

Muratie
MAP P. 128

TEL: 021 882 2330/6
TASTINGS/SALES:
    MON–FRI 09:00–17:00
    SAT 10:00–16:00
TOURS: BY APPOINTMENT
RESTAURANT: NO
PICNICS: NO
ACCOMMODATION: NO

The Farm Stall at Spier caters for picnickers.

Dining is an essential part of a visit to the winelands.

Ken Forrester's restaurant, 96 Winery Road.

The barrel cellar at Steenberg.

Neil Ellis — MAP P. 126
TEL: 021 887 0649
TASTINGS/SALES:
  MON–FRI 09:30–16:30
  SAT 10:00–14:00
TOURS: NO
RESTAURANT: NO
PICNICS: NO
ACCOMMODATION: NO

Rust en Vrede — MAP P. 126
TEL: 021 881 3881
TASTINGS/SALES:
  MON–FRI 09:00–17:00
  OCT–APR, SAT 09:00–16:00
  MAY–SEP, SAT 09:00–15:00
TOURS: YES
RESTAURANT: NO
PICNICS: NO
ACCOMMODATION: NO

Saxenburg — MAP P. 130
TEL: 021 903 6113
TASTINGS/SALES:
  MON–FRI 09:00–17:00
  SAT 09:00–16:00
  SUN 10:00–16:00
TOURS: BY APPOINTMENT
RESTAURANT:
  GUINEA FOWL TEL 021 906 5232
  LUNCH WED–MON
  DINNER WED–SAT
PICNICS: BASKETS AVAILABLE
ACCOMMODATION: NO

Simonsig — MAP P. 132
TEL: 021 888 4900 / 4915
TASTINGS/SALES:
  MON–FRI 08:30–17:00
  SAT 08:30–16:00
TOURS: BY APPOINTMENT
RESTAURANT: NO
PICNICS: BRING YOUR OWN
ACCOMMODATION:
  PALM COTTAGE, MORGENSTER FARM,
  VLOTTENBURG TEL 021 883 2881

Spier — MAP P. 130
TEL: 021 809 1146 / 1190
TASTINGS/SALES:
  MON–SUN 09:00–17:00
TOURS: BY APPOINTMENT
RESTAURANTS:
  JONKERSHUIS, TAPHUIS, FIGARO'S, TOTO'S,
  FARM STALL
  TEL 021 809 1100
  LUNCH 12:30–15:30; DINNER 18:00–22:00
PICNICS: BASKETS AVAILABLE AT FARM STALL
ACCOMMODATION:
  HOTEL TEL 021 809 1155

Sylvanvale — MAP P. 130
TEL: 021 865 2012
TASTINGS/SALES:
  MON–SUN 07:00–08:00
TOURS: BY APPOINTMENT
RESTAURANT: VINELEAF (TEL AS ABOVE)
  MON–SUN 07:00–22:00
PICNICS: BASKETS AVAILABLE BY
  ARRANGEMENT
ACCOMMODATION:
  DEVON VALLEY HOTEL (TEL AS ABOVE)

Rustenberg — MAP P. 128
TEL: 021 809 1200
TASTINGS/SALES:
  MON–FRI 09:00–16:30
  SAT 09:00–12:30
TOURS: NO
RESTAURANT: NO
PICNICS: NO
ACCOMMODATION: NO

Thelema — MAP P. 128
TEL: 021 885 1924
TASTINGS/SALES:
  MON–FRI 09:00–17:00
  SAT 09:00–13:00
TOURS: NO
RESTAURANT: NO
PICNICS: NO
ACCOMMODATION: NO

Villiera — MAP PP. 132, 136
TEL: 021 882 2002/3
TASTINGS/SALES:
  MON–FRI 08:30–17:00
  SAT 08:30–13:00
TOURS: SELF GUIDED
RESTAURANT: NO
PICNICS: BRING YOUR OWN
ACCOMMODATION: NO

Vredenheim — MAP P. 130
TEL: 021 881 3878
TASTINGS/SALES:
  MON–FRI 09:00–17:00
  SAT 09:30–14:00
TOURS: NO
RESTAURANT:
  BARRIQUE TEL 021 881 3001
  TUE–SUN 12:00–14:30, 18:30–22:00
PICNICS: NO
ACCOMMODATION: NO

Warwick — MAP P. 128
TEL: 021 884 4410
TASTINGS/SALES:
  NOV–APR, MON–FRI 10:00–16:00; SAT 09:00–13:00
TOURS: BY APPOINTMENT
RESTAURANT: NO
PICNICS: BASKETS AVAILABLE BY
  ARRANGEMENT OR BRING YOUR OWN
ACCOMMODATION: NO

Welmoed — MAP P. 130
TEL: 021 881 3870
TASTINGS/SALES:
  MON–FRI 09:00–17:30
  SAT 09:00–17:00
  SUN 10:00–16:00
TOURS: BY APPOINTMENT
RESTAURANT:
  THE DUCK POND TEL 021 881 3310
  LUNCH ONLY
PICNICS: NO
ACCOMMODATION: NO

Zevenwacht — MAP P. 130
TEL: 021 903 5123
TASTINGS/SALES:
  MON–FRI 08:30–17:00
  SAT & SUN 09:30–17:00
TOURS: BY APPOINTMENT
RESTAURANT: TEL AS ABOVE
  B'FAST, LUNCH & DINNER
PICNICS: BASKETS AVAILABLE
ACCOMMODATION:
  COUNTRY INN TEL 021 906 1570

Ashanti — MAP P. 136
TEL: 021 862 0789
TASTINGS/SALES:
  MON–FRI 10:00–16:45
  SAT 10:00–16:00
  IN SEASON, SUN 10:00–16:00
TOURS: BY APPOINTMENT, WEEKDAYS ONLY
RESTAURANT:
  IL CASALE TEL 021 862 6288
PICNICS: NO
ACCOMMODATION: NO

Backsberg — MAP PP. 128, 136
TEL: 021 875 5141
TASTINGS/SALES:
  MON–FRI 08:30–17:00
  SAT 09:00–14:00
  SUN 11:00–15:00
TOURS:
  SELF GUIDED
  BY APPOINTMENT FOR GROUPS OF 10 OR
  MORE
RESTAURANT: TEL AS ABOVE
  MON–FRI 10:00–16:00
  SAT & SUN 11:00–15:00
PICNICS: BRING YOUR OWN
ACCOMMODATION: NO

Fairview — MAP P. 136
TEL: 021 863 2450
TASTINGS/SALES:
  MON–FRI 08:30–17:00
  SAT 08:30–13:00
TOURS: NO
RESTAURANT: NO
PICNICS: NO
ACCOMMODATION: NO

Glen Carlou — MAP PP. 128, 136
TEL: 021 875 5528/96
TASTINGS/SALES:
  MON–FRI 08:45–16:45
  SAT 09:00–12:45
TOURS: BY APPOINTMENT
RESTAURANT: NO
PICNICS: NO
ACCOMMODATION: NO

Hoopenburg
MAP P. 136

TEL: 021 884 4221/2
TASTINGS/SALES:
MON–FRI 09:00–17:00
SAT 09:30–13:00
TOURS: BY APPOINTMENT
RESTAURANT: NO
PICNICS: NO
ACCOMMODATION: NO

Nelson's Creek
MAP P. 138

TEL: 021 863 8453
TASTINGS/SALES:
MON–FRI 08:00–17:00
SAT 09:00–13:00
TOURS: BY APPOINTMENT
RESTAURANT:
RIX AT THE CREEK TEL 083 632 5276
PICNICS: BASKETS AVAILABLE
ACCOMMODATION: NO

Rhebokskloof
MAP P. 138

TEL: 021 869 8386
TASTINGS/SALES:
MON–SUN 09:00–17:00
TOURS: BY APPOINTMENT
RESTAURANT: TEL 021 869 8606
LUNCH MON–SUN
DINNER THU–MON
PICNICS: NO
ACCOMMODATION: NO

Ruitersvlei
MAP P. 136

TEL: 021 863 1517
TASTINGS/SALES:
MON–FRI 08:30–17:30
SAT 09:00–14:00
TOURS: NO
RESTAURANT:
BISTRO TEL 021 863 3959
LUNCH & DINNER TUE–SUN
PICNICS: NO
ACCOMMODATION: NO

Seidelberg
MAP P. 136

TEL: 021 863 3495
TASTINGS/SALES:
MON–FRI 09:00–17:30
SAT & SUN 10:00–16:00
TOURS: BY APPOINTMENT
RESTAURANT:
OLIVE & VINE (TEL AS ABOVE)
MON–FRI 10,00–16:00
SAT & SUN 10:00–15:00
PICNICS: BASKETS AVAILABLE
ACCOMMODATION: NO

Welgemeend
MAP P. 136

TEL: 021 875 5210
TASTINGS/SALES:
WED 14:00–16:00
SAT 09:00–12:30
TOURS: BY APPOINTMENT
RESTAURANT: NO
PICNICS: NO
ACCOMMODATION: NO

Agusta
MAP P. 145

TEL: 021 876 3195
TASTINGS/SALES:
MON–SUN 10:00–18:00
TOURS: BY APPOINTMENT
RESTAURANT:
LA PROVENÇAL TEL 021 876 2065
PICNICS: NO
ACCOMMODATION:
GRAND PROVENCE GUEST HOUSE
TEL 021 876 2163

Boschendal
MAP P. 128

TEL: 021 870 4211 / 4226
TASTINGS/SALES:
NOV–APR, MON–FRI 08:30–16:30; SAT 09:00–12:30
MAY–OCT, MON–SAT 08:30–16:30
TOURS: BY APPOINTMENT
RESTAURANT:
BOSCHENDAL RESTAURANT TEL 021 870 4273/4
BUFFET LUNCH 12:00 (BOOKING ESSENTIAL)
LE CAFÉ TEL 021 870 4273/4
MON–SUN 10:00–17:00
PICNICS: NOV–APR, BASKETS AVAILABLE AT LE
PIQUE NIQUE
ACCOMMODATION: NO

Cabrière
MAP P. 145

TEL: 021 876 2630
TASTINGS/SALES:
MON–FRI 08:30–17:00
SAT 10:30–14:00
TOURS: SAT 11:00 OR BY APPOINTMENT
RESTAURANT:
HAUTE CABRIÉRE CELLAR TEL 021 876 3688
IN SEASON, LUNCH MON–SUN; DINNER
WED–MON
OUT OF SEASON, DINNER FRI & SAT
PICNICS: NO
ACCOMMODATION: NO

Chamonix
MAP P. 145

TEL: 021 876 2494
TASTINGS/SALES:
MON–SUN 09:00–17:00
TOURS: BY APPOINTMENT
RESTAURANT:
LA MAISON DE CHAMONIX TEL 021 876 2393
TUE–SUN 12:30–17:00; FRI 18:00–23:00
PICNICS: NO
ACCOMMODATION:
CAPE CHAMONIX GUEST HOUSES

Dieu Donné
MAP P. 145

TEL: 021 876 2493
TASTINGS/SALES:
MON–FRI 08:30–16:30
TOURS: BY APPOINTMENT
RESTAURANT: NO
PICNICS: BRING YOUR OWN
ACCOMMODATION: NO

La Couronne
MAP P. 145

TEL: 021 876 3939
TASTINGS/SALES:
IN SEASON, MON–SUN 10:00–16:00
TOURS:
IN SEASON
BY APPOINTMENT OUT OF SEASON
RESTAURANT: TEL 021 876 2770
PICNICS: BASKETS AVAILABLE
ACCOMMODATION:
HOTEL TEL 021 876 2770

La Motte
MAP P. 145

TEL: 021 876 3119
TASTINGS/SALES:
MON–FRI 09:00–16:30
SAT 09:00–12:00
TOURS: BY APPOINTMENT
RESTAURANT: NO
PICNICS: NO
ACCOMMODATION: NO

Mont Rochelle
MAP P. 145

TEL: 021 876 3000
TASTINGS/SALES:
SEP–APR, MON–SUN 11:00–17:00
MAY–AUG, MON–SAT 11:00–17:00
TOURS: DAILY 11:00, 12:30 & 15:00
RESTAURANT: NO
PICNICS: BASKETS AVAILABLE
ACCOMMODATION: NO

Môreson
MAP P. 145

TEL: 021 876 3055
TASTINGS/SALES:
NOV–APR, TUE–SUN 11:00–17:00
MAY–OCT, WED–SUN 11:00–16:00
TOURS: BY APPOINTMENT
RESTAURANT:
BREAD & WINE TEL 021 876 3692
DAILY 12:00–17:00
PICNICS: NO
ACCOMMODATION: NO

Plaisir de Merle
MAP P. 128

TEL: 021 874 1071/2
TASTINGS/SALES:
MON–FRI 09:00–17:00
SAT 10:00–13:00
TOURS: BY APPOINTMENT
RESTAURANT: NO
PICNICS: BRING YOUR OWN
ACCOMMODATION: NO

Stony Brook
MAP P. 145

TEL: 021 876 2182
TASTINGS/SALES:
MON–SAT 09:00–13:00
AFTER 13:00 BY APPOINTMENT
TOURS: NO
RESTAURANT: NO
PICNICS: NO
ACCOMMODATION: NO

Avontuur
MAP P. 134

TEL: 021 855 3450
TASTINGS/SALES:
MON–FRI 09:00–16:30
SAT 09:00–13:00
TOURS: NO
RESTAURANT: TEL AS ABOVE
PICNICS: NO
ACCOMMODATION: NO

Eikendal
MAP P. 134

TEL: 021 855 1422
TASTINGS/SALES:
MON–FRI 09:00–17:00
MAY–SEP, SAT 09:00–13:00
OCT–APR, SAT 09:00–16:00
SUN 10:30–16:00
TOURS:
DEC–FEB, MON–FRI 11:30 & 14:30
BY APPOINTMENT FOR GROUPS OF 10 OR
MORE
RESTAURANT: TEL AS ABOVE
OCT–APR, MON–FRI 12:00–14:00
MID-NOV–MID-APR, SUN 12:00–14:00
PICNICS: BASKETS AVAILABLE
ACCOMMODATION:
EIKENDAL LODGE TEL 021 855 3617

Helderberg
MAP P. 134

TEL: 021 842 2371
TASTINGS/SALES:
MON–FRI 09:00–17:30
SAT 09:00–17:00
TOURS: BY APPOINTMENT
RESTAURANT: TEL 021 842 2012
LUNCH MON–SAT
PICNICS: NO
ACCOMMODATION: NO

J. P. Bredell
MAP P. 134

TEL: 021 842 2478
TASTINGS/SALES:
MON–FRI 08:00–17:00
TOURS: NO
RESTAURANT: NO
PICNICS: NO
ACCOMMODATION: NO

Morgenster
MAP P. 134

TEL: 021 852 1738
TASTINGS/SALES:
TASTINGS BY APPOINTMENT
SALES MON–FRI 10:00–17:00
TOURS: BY APPOINTMENT
RESTAURANT: NO
PICNICS: NO
ACCOMMODATION: NO

Somerbosch
MAP P. 134

TEL: 021 855 3615
TASTINGS/SALES:
MON–FRI 09:00–17:00
SAT 09:00–13:00
TOURS: BY APPOINTMENT
RESTAURANT: NO
PICNICS: NO
ACCOMMODATION: NO

Stonewall
MAP P. 134

TEL: 083 310 2407
TASTINGS/SALES:
DEC–JAN, MON–FRI 09:00–17:00; SAT 09:00–13:00
TOURS: BY APPOINTMENT
RESTAURANT: NO
PICNICS: NO
ACCOMMODATION: NO

Vergelegen
MAP P. 134

TEL: 021 847 1334
TASTINGS/SALES:
MON–SUN 09:30–16:00
MAY–OCT, CLOSED SUN
TOURS: BY APPOINTMENT
RESTAURANT:
LADY PHILLIPS TEL 021 847 1346
TEA & LUNCH
THE ROSE TERRACE NOV–APR
TEL 021 847 1346
LUNCH ONLY
PICNICS: BASKETS AVAILABLE
ACCOMMODATION: NO

Yonder Hill
MAP P. 134

TEL: 021 855 1008
TASTINGS/SALES:
MON–FRI 09:00–16:00
TOURS: BY APPOINTMENT
RESTAURANT: NO
PICNICS: NO
ACCOMMODATION: NO

Index

Page numbers in *italic* indicate photographs